A Letter from Your Child:

What Your Kid Wishes You Knew About

A Workbook for Parents

Stop Yelling, Understand Your Child, Build Stronger Connections, and Raise Emotionally Healthy Kids.

CARRIE KHANG

© Copyright Carrie Khang 2024 - All rights reserved.

The content contained within this book may not be reproduced, duplicated or transmitted without direct written permission from the author or the publisher.

Under no circumstances will any blame or legal responsibility be held against the publisher, or author, for any damages, reparation, or monetary loss due to the information contained within this book. Either directly or indirectly. You are responsible for your own choices, actions, and results.

Legal Notice:

This book is copyright protected. This book is only for personal use. You cannot amend, distribute, sell, use, quote or paraphrase any part, or the content within

Disclaimer Notice:

Please note the information contained within this document is for educational and entertainment purposes only. All effort has been executed to present accurate, up to date, and reliable, complete information. No warranties of any kind are declared or implied. Readers acknowledge that the author is not engaging in the rendering of legal, financial, medical or professional advice. The content within this book has been derived from various sources. Please consult a licensed professional before attempting any techniques outlined in this book.

By reading this document, the reader agrees that under no circumstances is the author responsible for any losses, direct or indirect, which are incurred as a result of the use of the information contained within this document, including, but not limited to, — errors, omissions, or inaccuracies.

Before You Begin, grab your *gift!*

Because parenting is hard, and you're doing the work. I've put together a collection of practical tools to support you beyond this book.

🎁 From calming strategies to printable activities for your kids, these bonus resources are yours, completely free!

📱 Scan the QR code

📦 Includes:
- ✔ *Top 10 Yelling Triggers*
- ✔ *7-Day Self-Care for Moms*
- ✔ *5-Minute Gratitude Journal for Kids*
- ✔ *How do I? Printable Worksheet*
- ✔ *The Gratitude Journal for Moms*

https://carriekhang.com

Other Books by Carrie Khang:

Table of Contents

Introduction xii
Ch1: Love Me for Me 17
    Comparison Hurts *18*
    Impact on Self-Esteem *18*
    Activity: "Uniquely Me" Poster *26*
CH2: Warm Looks, Please 29
    From Negativity to Connection *30*
    Five Steps to Positivity *30*
    Activity: "Mirror Game" *38*
CH3: Listen to Me 41
    Actively Listening to Your Child *42*
    Please Don't *43*
    Activity: Story Jar *51*
CH4: Don't Scold Me in Public 55
    Scolding isn't a Public Affair *56*
    What to Do if You've Publicly Scolded Your Child *58*
    Activity: Calm Conversation Corner *65*
CH5: Help Me Understand My Feelings 67
    Be My Emotional Compass *68*
    Child Brain Development *70*
    How to Model Healthy Emotional Responses *71*
    Activity: Emotional Wheel *78*
CH6: Your Apology Matters to Me 81
    Saying Sorry the Right Way *82*
    Laura and Mia's Story *84*

  Encouraging Your Child to Apologize 85
  Activity: Apology Role-Playing 89

CH7: Teach Me Gently 93
  Rethinking Discipline 94
  Are You Missing Teachable Moments? 95
  Activity: Plan for Positivity 103

CH8: No Yelling Zone 107
  Avoiding Frustration 108
  How to Connect with Your Child 109
  Activity: Practicing "I" Statements 118

CH9: Peel Off the Labels 122
  Choose Your Words Wisely 123
  Watch Out for Unintentional Labels 124
  Activity: "My Strengths Collage" 131

CH10: Help Me Follow the Rules 133
  Why Boundaries Matter 134
  How Differing Parenting Styles Confuse Kids 135
  Setting Effective Boundaries 136
  Activity: "Family Rules Board" 143

CH11: Let Me Do It! 145
  What Is Your Parenting Style? 146
  Encouraging Independence 148
  Managing Parental Anxiety 149
  Activity: "I Can Do It!" Chart 155

CH12: Promises Matter 157
  Keeping Your Word 158
  Practical Tips for Keeping Promises 160
  Activity: The Promise Jar 166

CH13: Let's Play! 169
  Quality Time, Happy Kid 170
  The Importance of Quality Time 171
  Overcoming Common Challenges 172
  Tips for Integrating Playtime 174
  Activity: Our Playtime Plan 182

CH14: Fair Consequences 185
    Setting Reasonable Consequences................................ *186*
    Hassan and Amir's Story.. *188*
    How to Teach Through Consequences *190*
    Activity: "Cause and Effect" Cards *194*

CH15: Screen Time Struggles 197
    Understanding the Issue *198*
    Taming Excessive Electronic Use................................ *199*
    How to Earn Screen Time *201*
    Activity 1: Screen-Free Fun... *208*

Reflection 212

Conclusion 215

Resources 219

"Don't worry that children never listen to you; worry that they are always watching you."

— *Robert Fulghum*

Introduction

"To be in your children's memories tomorrow, you have to be in their lives today." – Barbara Johnson

Hey, fellow parents!

Let's get real for a moment. Parenting? It's a wild ride. One minute you're marveling at the little person you've brought into the world, and the next, you're trying to figure out how to get crayon marks off the couch cushions. We all want to raise amazing humans, but in the chaos of daily life—juggling work, keeping the peace, and maybe finding a moment for ourselves—it's easy to lose sight of what really matters.

Think of this book as a wake-up call from those little folks we're trying so hard to guide. It's not about the messes, the missed recitals, or the bedtime battles. It's about the heart and soul of parenting—connecting with our kids on a level that goes way beyond the surface.

Throughout this book, you'll find 15 heartfelt messages from your child. They're the real deal—the everyday moments that might seem small but are huge to your little one. As you read, you'll recall the times your child tried something new and looked up to see if you were watching, the moments they messed up and needed to know it was okay, and those quiet talks that assured them you're on their team, no matter what.

Each chapter is accompanied by *Quiet Time* worksheets designed to help you learn more about yourself and your child. By reflecting on your own childhood and connecting it to your current parenting methods, you will become the parent you want to be—and the parent your child needs you to be. So, make sure to set aside time to fill out the worksheets.

Loving our kids unconditionally means celebrating their unique sparks. Your child might not be the next Mozart or a star athlete—and that's perfectly fine. He might be the one who spends hours lost in a book, invent the best indoor games on a rainy day, or have the empathy of a saint. Each child shines in their own way and on their own time. Our job? It's to be there with a patient heart and open arms, ready to cheer them on when their moment comes—whatever that moment looks like.

Here's the thing: taking things personally or expecting our kids to see the world from our grown-up vantage point is a recipe for frustration. Remember, we're the adults. We've got the big-picture view, but they're just getting to know this thing called life. Their world is up close and immediate, filled with wonders we've forgotten to notice. Judging their actions through our adult lens doesn't just miss the mark; it's not playing fair.

Kids grow best under the sunshine of our attention and the rain of our love—unconditional, unwavering, and understanding. It's about getting down to their eye level, literally and figuratively, and seeing the world as they do. It's about embracing their curiosity, their boundless energy—and yes, even their tantrums(!)—as part of the journey.

So, as you read through A Letter from Your Child, let it remind you of the little things—like how a hug can fix a bad day, how listening to a story about dragons can be the best part of your evening, and how saying sorry when you mess up can teach more about respect and love than any lecture.

Let's promise to fill our days with more patience, more understanding, and more willingness to let our kids guide us sometimes. Because when we love them for who they are, not who we think they should be, we're not just raising kids; we're nurturing future adults who know love, respect, and empathy firsthand.

Here's to the journey, the mess, and the magic of parenthood. Let's do this together, with love.

CHAPTER 1

Love Me for Me

"Every child is a different kind of flower, and all together, they make this world a beautiful garden." —Unknown

I'm not Brendon, who lives next door, or Jacob, who can swim super, super fast. I'm just me! I love making funny faces, asking a bazillion times why the sky is blue, and dancing like nobody's watching in our living room. When you love me for who I am, I can touch the stars.

Your child is one of a kind—and that's something worth celebrating! In this chapter, we will explore the beauty of their individuality and the dangers of comparing them to others. When you take time to understand and nurture your little one's uniqueness, you'll watch their self-esteem and happiness bloom.

Comparison Hurts

Think about the last time you compared your child to someone else. Was it an attempt to motivate them? Maybe you were trying to reassure yourself that they're reaching milestones. Whatever the reason, put yourself in their place for a moment. Imagine your child making comments like, *"Jason's mom isn't overweight,"* or, *"Milo's dad is great at baseball."* Feeling insecure yet? Your child feels the same way! Comparisons can make them feel like they aren't good enough, leading to low self-esteem, ongoing insecurity, and unhealthy competition.

Impact on Self-Esteem

When kids are constantly compared to others, they start to believe they're not good enough. Comparisons plant a seed of doubt that can severely damage their self-esteem, making them feel like they'll never measure up. This can even keep children from trying their best. If you frequently ask your little one, *"Why can't you be more like your sister? She always gets straight A's,"* they may begin to wonder, *"What's the point in giving my all at school if I'm not smart enough to make good grades anyway?"*

- ## Under Pressure

Every kid is different expecting them to be just like someone else is an unrealistic expectation that can cause stress, anxiety, and fear. Forcing your child into unwanted competition with others can make them feel like they have to struggle to gain your approval. This can cause them to become overly cautious and less willing to take risks, hurting their personal growth and development.

- ## Strained Relationships

Comparisons can hurt relationships. A child who feels they are constantly being measured against a sibling or peer may begin to resent that person—and the parent making the comparison. This is a recipe for disaster for the entire family dynamic and can lead to jealousy, broken trust, and a lack of communication.

Emily and Sam's Story

Emily, a mother of two boys, often compared her younger son Sam to his older brother Jake. Sam enjoyed reading and was a talented artist, while Jake excelled at sports. Emily, who had been an athlete herself, often pleaded with Sam to follow in Jake's footsteps. This made Sam feel inadequate, like his talents were worthless. Eventually, Sam confided in Emily about feeling like he was always in Jake's shadow. *"Mom, it doesn't seem like you care at all about the things I am good at,"* Sam said, pain in his voice. *"All that matters are Jake's sports, so why should I even try?"*

Emily felt ashamed. She hadn't even thought about how her comparisons were hurting Sam. She knew she needed to make a change.

Unsure of how to encourage Sam, Emily found herself deep in reflection. She realized that, just like roses on the same bush, both of her children were beautiful and unique in their special ways. Emily decided to start focusing on nurturing each of her children's unique gifts instead of comparing them. She turned to books and the internet for healthy ways to support her youngest son.

Recognizing Sam's talent for drawing, Emily set up a small art corner for him and proudly displayed his artwork around the house. She explored Sam's knack for storytelling and encouraged him to share his tales with the family. While taking these steps, she also encouraged Jake to recognize Sam's efforts. Initially, Sam was hesitant, but Emily pressed on. She watched as his confidence grew each day with consistent praise and support.

One evening, Sam proudly presented a storybook he had created, and the whole family applauded. Seeing Jake genuinely appreciate his work, Sam's face lit up with pride. His self-esteem soared, and

the change brought the brothers closer, helping them appreciate each other's unique strengths.

Quiet Time

Reflecting on the Past and Present

1. Did your parents ever compare you to your siblings or friends when you were younger? What did they usually compare? How did it make you feel at the time? (Feel free to write your thoughts.)

   _____
   _____
   _____
   _____

2. How did those comparisons from your parents affect your relationship with them? Did it create distance or bring you closer in any way?

   _____
   _____
   _____
   _____

3. Have you ever caught yourself comparing your child to others? Who did you compare them to, and what was it about? How did your child react afterward?

4. Remember how comparisons from your parents made you feel? Now think about how the comparisons you make might affect your child. Have you seen any changes in their behavior or confidence because of it?

5. Was there any sibling rivalry in your home growing up? How did it affect your relationship with your siblings, and how do you handle it now with your kids?

6. When your parents compared you to others, was there one comment or action that stayed with you the most? How has it influenced the way you parent today?

Exploring Your Child's Unique Traits

1. What are five things that make your child special or different from other kids?

2. Can you think of a recent moment where your child's uniqueness really shined?

3. What's one family activity you could start that lets each child show off their own personality or skills?

4. How does your child show their creativity or unique way of thinking?

5. How can you help your child grow their unique talents and interests?

Celebrating Individuality

1. How can you celebrate what makes your child one of a kind?

2. What's one thing you can do to show your child you appreciate them just as they are? Could it be more praise, quality time, or something else?

3. Are there any family traditions or new activities you could start that highlight each of your children's individuality?

4. How can you help your child feel proud of their unique qualities?

 **activity: "Uniquely Me" Poster**

What You'll Need:

- A poster board
- Markers, crayons, or colored pencils
- Glue or tape
- Magazines, photos, or stickers

How to Do It:

Together with your child, create a "Uniquely Me" poster. Title the poster "Uniquely Me," and discuss with your little one all the things that make them special. Write these traits on the poster. Let your child decorate the poster with drawings, stickers, or magazine cutouts that represent their special qualities and interests. Hang the poster in a place your child will see it often for a confidence boost and a fun reminder of everything that make them special.

Why It's Helpful:

This chart highlights what makes your child special, boosts self-esteem by focusing on their unique traits, and serves as a fun way for your child to share their individuality.

Encouraging Consistency with Positive Phrases

- "You are amazing just the way you are."
- "I love how you always find a way to make me smile."
- "Your creativity and imagination are wonderful."
- "You don't have to be like anyone else; you're perfect as you are."
- "I'm so proud of you for being you."

Final Thoughts

Your child is unique and deserves to be appreciated for exactly who they are. By avoiding comparisons and focusing on their individual strengths, you can help your little one flourish into a confident and happy person. Celebrate their uniqueness and let them know they are loved just the way they are.

CHAPTER 2

Warm Looks, Please

"A loving look can make all the difference." —Unknown

When I get messy or accidentally scribble on the wall (whoopsie!), I know I'm a lot to handle. But when you look at me with kind eyes, it's like we're sharing a super warm hug without even touching.

The eyes are the window to the soul, and a look can say it all. In this chapter, we will learn about the importance of using warm and positive non-verbal communication with your child. Something as simple as how you look at your little one can make a huge difference in their emotional well-being and sense of security! By using affectionate and encouraging looks, you can foster a strong, trusting relationship with them.

From Negativity to Connection

Picture yourself in a work meeting: your boss is frowning and sighing loudly. The entire room is tense—everyone is on edge, trying not to trigger another frustrated sigh. He doesn't say a single word, but your boss's message of disapproval is loud and clear. Now, think about how you react to your child at home. When they spill water, wear mismatched socks, or break a dish, do you unconsciously cross your arms, furrow your brow, or give an angry look?

Many parents don't realize that their default body language often communicates negativity. It's easy to slip into habits like folding your arms or giving an unfriendly glare without noticing. Imagine setting up a camera and watching how you react to your child. You might be shocked to see how often you appear cold or unapproachable! Even if you don't intend for them to, these non-verbal cues can create an atmosphere of fear and anxiety for your child.

Five Steps to Positivity

1. Smile and Offer Help

When your child makes a mistake, swap your frown for a smile. For instance, if your little one knocks over a glass of milk, instead of sighing in frustration, smile and say, *"That's okay—accidents happen. Let's clean it up together."* This shows them that mistakes are a part of learning, and you're there to support them. With this approach, you trade a potentially hurtful memory for a bonding moment.

2. Practice Open and Relaxed Body Language

Keep your arms uncrossed, maintain a relaxed posture, and use gentle eye contact. Imagine your child coming to you with a broken toy. Rather than closing your posture and scowling, lean down to their level, make soft eye contact, and speak tenderly. This openness makes you more approachable and signals to your child that they can come to you with their problems, reassuring them you're their safe space.

3. Encourage with Nods and Smiles

When your child makes an effort to solve a problem, even if they don't succeed, encourage them with friendly nods and smiles. For example, if they try to tie their shoes and struggle, give them a nod of encouragement and a caring smile, saying, *"You're doing great—keep trying!"* This positive reinforcement boosts their confidence and motivates them to keep at it.

4. Practice Patience and Understanding

Take a deep breath and calm yourself before reacting to your child's behavior. Let's say they accidentally spill paint on the floor. Resist the urge to yell, take a moment to breathe, and then calmly help them clean up. Showing patience and understanding helps your child feel safe and secure, teaching them that you aren't just a source of discipline—you're their biggest supporter.

5. Express Empathy

Speak to your child how you'd want to be spoken to—choose kind words that show empathy and understanding. If they are sad because their Lego tower collapsed, don't brush it off. Instead, say, *"I see you worked hard on that. It's frustrating when things don't go as planned. Let's see how we can rebuild it together."* Kids need to know it's okay to feel upset when things don't work out. This attitude teaches them you're there to help them navigate their emotions.

By incorporating these small changes, you can create a positive, nurturing environment where your child feels loved and supported. This approach both strengthens your bond and fills your little one with a sense of security and confidence. Remember, your non-verbal cues are powerful tools in building your child's emotional well-being. Use them to create a strong, supportive connection that encourages your precious one to grow and thrive.

Mark and Lily's Story

Mark, the father of a young girl named Lily, often found himself frustrated when Lily made mistakes. His natural reaction was to frown or give her a harsh look. Over time, he noted that Lily was becoming more anxious and withdrawn, avoiding eye contact and hesitating to share her thoughts.

One evening, while putting Lily to bed, he noticed she was unusually quiet. When he asked her what was wrong, she hesitated. Her voice quivering, she said, *"Dad, I'm scared to tell you. You always look so angry when I mess up."* Lily pulled the covers up to her chin, turned over, and pretended to sleep.

Mark felt a pang of guilt. He hadn't realized how deeply his non-verbal cues affected Lily. As he lay in bed that night, Mark made a promise to change. He decided to experiment with more supportive body language.

It wasn't easy; his initial attempts felt awkward and forced. He often had to catch himself from scowling or crossing his arms. One morning, Lily spilled a glass of juice all over the kitchen table. Mark's first instinct was to scold her, but he caught himself. He took a deep breath and kneeled down to her level. *"It's okay. Accidents happen,"* he said with a smile. *"Let's clean it up together."*

At first, Lily was skeptical. She watched him cautiously as if expecting the old angry reaction to resurface. But as time went on and Mark consistently responded with patience and love when Lily made a mistake, she began to let her guard down. There were moments when Mark struggled to keep his cool, especially after a long day at work, but the echo of Lily's words motivated him to press on.

Gradually, Lily started to open up to Mark. Her fear of judgment slowly started to fade, and she began to excitedly share stories about her day and her feelings. One evening, she proudly showed Mark a drawing she made. A hint of doubt crept into Lily's mind, and she half expected her dad to criticize her. Instead, Mark showered her with praise, admiring her effort and creativity. Lily's face lit up with a smile, and for the first time in a while, Mark saw genuine confidence in her eyes.

Mark and Lily's journey was not without setbacks. There were days when he slipped back into old habits, and Lily would retreat into her shell. But with each misstep, Mark learned to forgive himself and try again. Over time, their relationship grew stronger, built on a foundation of trust and understanding.

Quiet Time

Reflecting on the Past and Present

1. When you were a kid, did your parents have certain looks or body language when they were angry? How did it make you feel?

2. How did your parents' non-verbal cues affect your emotions as a child? Did it ever make you feel scared, safe, or something else?

3. What kind of non-verbal signals do you give off when you're upset with your child? Do you cross your arms, give a certain look, or use another kind of body language?

4. Do you notice any similarities between your non-verbal habits and your parents' habits? What do you think about that?

5. How do you think your body language affects your child's feelings?

Practicing Positive Non-Verbal Communication

1. What's one small change you can make to your body language to show more support and love to your child? Maybe more smiles, softer eyes, or open arms?

2. Think about a time when your child needed reassurance. Did your body language help or make the situation harder? What would you do differently next time?

Building Stronger Connections

1. What can you do to make sure your body language always sends a message of love and support? Even on tough days, how can you keep it positive?

2. How can you make using positive body language a daily habit? Is there a small thing you can do every day, like reminding yourself to smile or give a comforting hug?

3. Write yourself a little reminder to keep your body language open and warm. What would you write? Something like, *"Smile first"* or *"Show kindness in your eyes"*?

🎯 Activity: "Mirror Game"

How to Do It:

Spend a few minutes playing the "Mirror Game" with your child. Stand in front of a mirror together and take turns making different facial expressions. You can try out emotions like happy, sad, surprised, frustrated, or silly. Don't forget to add in fun sounds and voices while making faces to keep the game engaging and lighthearted! Mimic each other's faces to see how they look. Talk about how each expression makes you feel and what it might communicate to someone else. For example, "How do you feel when you see a big smile? What about a sad face?" Next, talk about how expressing feelings can affect others to help build empathy and emotional recognition.

Why It's Helpful:

Learning to recognize and understand different emotions strengthens your child's emotional intelligence, and talking about emotions helps them learn to express themselves and understand others better. This game is playful, making it easy for kids to connect with their feelings.

Encouraging Consistency with Positive Phrases

- "I see you, and I care."
- "Your feelings matter to me."
- "I'm here for you, no matter what."
- "Let's figure this out together."
- "You are important to me."

Final Thoughts

Remember, your warm looks and gentle gestures have the power to nurture and reassure your child. It's the little things—a smile, a kind word, a gentle touch—that make them feel loved and secure. These moments of connection are the roots of trust and affection. Embrace the power of warmth in your everyday interactions and watch your child's confidence and happiness grow. Your loving presence is the greatest gift you can give them.

CHAPTER 3

Listen to Me

"Listening is where love begins: listening to ourselves and then to our neighbors." —Fred Rogers

When I talk about my day at school or the dragon I dreamed of, and you listen, my heart feels warm and fuzzy! Sometimes, I think you're too busy thinking about grown-up stuff. When you

ask me questions about the characters I imagine, I feel like my stories are as precious as treasure.

In this chapter, we'll explore the importance of truly listening to your child's stories. Active listening is a skill many of us have to learn—putting in the effort can help your little one feel valued and loved. Let's learn how to create a supportive and loving home by understanding and managing your responses to your child's words.

Actively Listening to Your Child

Imagine you're sharing something exciting or frustrating with your spouse. As you pour your heart out, you notice their eyes are glazed over—they're nodding occasionally, but they're not really engaging. You quietly stop talking and withdraw, feeling unappreciated and frustrated. Now, think about how this applies to your child. When they excitedly talk about their day at school or a dream they had, they need more than just a rushed nod or a distracted "okay." They need to see that you're genuinely interested in their stories.

Active listening involves fully focusing, understanding, responding, and remembering what your child says. It's not just about hearing the words but about engaging with the emotions and thoughts behind them. When you actively listen to your child, you're showing them that their thoughts and feelings are important to you. So put down your phone, make eye contact, and respond with genuine interest. Ask them questions that show you're curious about their world, like, *"What happened next?"* or, *"How did that make you feel?"* If you show them you care, you'll be amazed at how much more they open up!

Active listening is a little like magic—it can transform the exchange of words into meaningful connections. Imagine the joy on your child's face when they see you're completely focused on what they're saying. They'll be so excited to share more that you'll find them talking about all sorts of things, from their school day to their imaginary adventures. This makes them feel loved and is a huge confidence boost!

By simply listening to your child, you'll get to know the real them. This can change what you thought you knew about them, revealing talents you didn't even know they had. Just like all of us, kids feel they matter when their ideas, feelings, and abilities are treated with respect. Next time your child shares a story, show them their voice matters by listening with your heart. You'll watch their confidence and self-worth soar as they learn to understand and communicate what they feel, want, and need.

Please Don't

- ### Don't Be Critical of What Your Child Says

Show empathy and compassion when your child comes to you with a problem or mistake—don't immediately jump to criticism. Imagine them telling you they accidentally broke a vase. Instead of angrily snapping, *"Why are you always so careless?"* try listening to the whole story. Respond with understanding to help them feel safe to share with you next time.

- **Don't Jump to Lecture**

It can be easy to go into lecture mode when your youngster does something wrong. For instance, if they forget to do their homework, instead of lecturing them about responsibility, simply talk to them. Ask them how their day went and listen to their reasons for not completing the task. This gives them a chance to tell their side of the story and helps them feel heard before you give advice or set expectations.

- **Don't Try to Fix Everything for Your Child**

As parents, we naturally want to solve our kids' problems. But stepping in too quickly can hurt more than help, even preventing them from learning important skills. If your little one is struggling with a school project, resist the urge to do it for them. Instead, sit down together, discuss the problem, and help them figure out a solution. This approach encourages independence and problem-solving skills—and gives your child a sense of accomplishment.

Sarah and Ella's Story

Meet Sarah and her daughter Ella. Sarah, a busy working mom, often found herself listening to Ella's stories with half an ear while cooking dinner or checking emails. After a while, feeling that her stories weren't important, Ella started keeping them to herself. She began to wonder if something was wrong with her—why couldn't she keep her mother's attention?

One evening, as bedtime approached, Ella asked, *"Mom, did you buy the crayons that I asked you about? I need them for my science project on Monday."* Caught by surprise, Sarah replied, *"When did you ask me to buy crayons?"*

Ella's eyes filled with tears as she said, *"I told you a couple of times already, and you said 'yes.' See—you never listen. You don't even remember me telling you about the project. You're always like this."* She started to cry.

Sarah froze, suddenly realizing how inattentive she'd been—she didn't even remember Ella mentioning a science project. She recalled the lonely feeling she had when her mother was too busy to pay attention to her as a child. Seeing how much hurt she had caused by ignoring Ella's interests, Sarah knew she had to change.

Sarah hugged her child and apologized. Determined to make things right, she immediately went out to buy the crayons—but more importantly, she vowed to truly listen to Ella from that moment on. She started by setting aside 15 minutes each evening right after dinner as "Ella time," where she put away all distractions and gave her daughter her full attention. The first few days were tough—Sarah struggled to keep her mind from wandering, and Ella was hesitant to speak up.

Sarah began by asking open-ended questions about Ella's day, showing genuine interest in her stories. *"What was the best part of your day?"* she'd ask, or *"Can you tell me more about the purple dragon?"*

Initially, Ella's responses were short. But as days turned into weeks, Sarah's consistent effort started to pay off. Ella began to open up more, her stories becoming longer and more detailed. One evening, she shared an elaborate tale about dragons, complete with different characters and plotlines. Sarah listened intently, asking about every twist and turn, genuinely fascinated by Ella's imagination. She hadn't realized her daughter was so creative!

Ella's face lit up with joy, and Sarah realized the importance of these special moments. Their bond grew stronger, and Ella's confidence blossomed. Sarah learned that truly listening made Ella feel valued and understood. It was a gradual process, but the effort was worth it, bringing them closer than ever.

Quiet Time

Reflecting on the Past and Present

1. When you were a kid, did your parents really listen to your stories, or were they distracted? How did that make you feel when they didn't pay attention?

2. Do you think the way your parents listened (or didn't listen) to you influences how you listen to your child today? In what ways do you see this?

Practicing Active Listening

1. Think about the last story your child told you. What were the main points? How did you respond? Did you show interest, or were you a bit distracted?

2. How can you improve your listening skills after reflecting on that last conversation? What's one thing you can do differently next time?

3. What steps can you take to make sure you really listen to your child in the future? Is it putting your phone away or giving them your full attention?

Encouraging Storytelling and Bonding

1. What are five things your child loves to talk about? How can you use those topics to encourage more storytelling and bonding?

2. Does your child have a favorite story or character they talk about a lot? How about creating your own story with them, using those characters and themes? It's a fun way to bond!

_____
_____
_____

Creating Open Communication

1. Look at your daily routine. When can you carve out a little time just to listen to your child with no distractions??

_____
_____
_____

2. Pick specific times of the day when you'll focus entirely on your child's stories. Maybe during dinner or right before bedtime—whatever works best!

_____
_____
_____

Improving Listening Skills

1. What things usually distract you when your child is talking? How can you minimize those distractions to be more present in the conversation?

2. How can you show more enthusiasm when your child is sharing something with you? Whether it's asking follow-up questions or showing excitement, how can you let them know you care?

activity: story jar

What You'll Need:

- A jar
- Paper
- Pens, markers, colored pencils, or crayons
- Stickers
- Glue or tape
- Scissors

How to Do It:

Let your child decorate a jar with fun and colorful stickers or have them make some creative drawings and glue or tape them to the jar. Cut a piece of paper into strips. Whenever your child tells a story, write a short title on a strip of paper, fold it, and add it to the jar. Once a month, pull out a slip from the jar, retell the story, and discuss it together. Give it a creative spin by making a game out of it—challenge yourselves by adding to the story you pick out of the jar.

Why It's Helpful:

This activity makes storytelling fun and memorable while encouraging regular sharing and bonding. It also helps your child get in touch with their creative side.

Positive Phrases to Promote Active Listening

- "Tell me more about that!"
- "You tell such interesting stories!"
- "What happened next?"
- "That sounds exciting! How did it make you feel?"
- "Wow, I never knew that! Thanks for sharing."
- "I love listening to you talk. You're so interesting!"
- "You're so creative! I can't wait to hear more."
- "That must have been fun! Can you give me more details?"
- "It sounds like you had a great time. What was your favorite part?"
- "I appreciate you telling me about this. It's really important to me."
- "You have such a vivid imagination. It's amazing!"
- "That must have been a big moment for you. How did you handle it?"
- "I'm here and listening. Your story matters to me."
- "Your ideas are always so interesting. I'm glad you're sharing them with me."
- "Thank you for sharing this with me. It helps me understand you better."

Final Thoughts

Active listening is the key that opens the door to your child's world. It shows them they are seen, heard, and valued. When you listen with your heart, you're not just hearing words; you're connecting on a deeper level. Next time your child shares a story, pause, look into their eyes, and journey into their world. To your little one, your attentive presence is the greatest prize—moments you spend truly listening are ones they will cherish forever.

CHAPTER 4

Don't Scold Me in Public

"Speak quietly to a child in private; their heart will listen and their dignity will remain intact." —Anonymous

If I mess up, please don't scold me in front of others. It embarrasses me and makes me feel small. Can we discuss it privately? I promise to listen, and I'll learn

better without the added embarrassment.

Public scolding can be humiliating for kids. It can hurt their feelings and self-esteem and even make them less willing to learn from their mistakes. In this chapter, we will talk about the importance of handling discipline privately and respectfully. By ensuring these conversations are private, we can create a safe environment that respects our children's dignity and encourages better listening.

Scolding isn't a Public Affair

Time for a tough exercise: Picture an innocent child like your own. Throughout the years, they grow into a deeply unhappy person—they feel unworthy, they don't respect themselves or others, and they're struggling through life. As a parent, just imagining such a scenario is heartbreaking, but the truth is that scolding kids in public can cause long-lasting harm to their feelings and confidence, leading to outcomes like this.

Think back to a time when you were called out in front of others—by a boss, a teacher, or even a family member. How did you feel? Chances are, it was a mix of embarrassment, shame, and maybe even anger. Even if your critic had a point, it likely didn't resonate with you. Instead of focusing on the lesson, you were probably only thinking about how others saw you at that moment.

Now, consider how this feels for a child. When kids are publicly scolded, it can shatter their confidence, making them feel unworthy and insignificant. Imagine your child knocking over a dinner plate at a family gathering. Food splatters across the floor, and the plate shatters. Your immediate reaction might be to tell them off in front of everyone. If you do this, the smashed plate won't be their only problem—they'll also be dealing with the embarrassment of being scolded in front of others. Instead of learning to be careful, they might learn to fear making mistakes.

Handling these situations privately changes the narrative. It shows your child that you respect their feelings and that their dignity is important to you. This approach creates a safe space where they can truly listen to what you're saying without the distraction of an audience. In the shelter of a one-on-one discussion, your little one can focus on understanding the mistake they made and how to improve, rather than being consumed by shame.

Public scolding can also lead to long-term negative effects, causing kids to develop anxiety, become more secretive, or rebel against authority. They might even start to believe they are incapable or unworthy, damaging their self-esteem and hurting future relationships.

As they grow into teenagers, the effects of public scolding become even bigger, taking the typical changes and pressures of adolescence and greatly magnifying them. This can cause these teens to struggle with low self-esteem and self-doubt, making them more likely to give in to peer pressure or engage in risky behaviors to feel accepted.

When you instead take your child aside and talk to them calmly, you practice respectful discipline. This emphasizes to them that mistakes are a part of learning and growing, and it builds a foundation of trust and respect—helping them grow into an emotionally healthy individual.

In short, avoiding public scolding helps kids feel confident and valued, which is crucial for their development and happiness. Next time something goes wrong in public, take a deep breath and resist the urge to impulsively scold. Instead, find a quiet moment to discuss the situation privately and calmly with your child. They'll appreciate your understanding, support, and effort to build a respectful relationship.

What to Do if You've Publicly Scolded Your Child

Mistakes happen. Taking ownership when you've publicly shamed your child can be tough and feel like a hit to your pride, but it's important to claim responsibility and take steps to repair the damage. Here's how:

- ### Step 1: Apologize Sincerely

Start with a heartfelt apology. Let your child know you messed up, that you recognize your mistake, and that you genuinely regret it. You might say, *"I'm very sorry for bringing that up in front of everyone. I should have waited to talk to you about it in private. It wasn't fair to you, and I really regret it."*

- ## Step 2: Communicate Assurance

Rebuild trust by assuring your child it won't happen again—and mean it. Explain how you plan to handle similar situations differently in the future with a phrase like, *"From now on, I promise to talk to you privately if there's a problem."*

- ## Step 3: Talk Openly

Have an honest conversation with your child about how your actions affected them. Be prepared to actively listen and take ownership without becoming defensive. Brainstorm together and agree on better ways to handle similar situations. Creating a signal your child can use if they feel embarrassed or upset in public can help you avoid another slip-up.

- ## Step 4: Rebuild Connection

Next, you should focus on repairing and strengthening your connection with your child. A great way to do this is by coming up with a few activities you can do together that show your little ones they are valued and loved. Some fun ideas are a special outing with just the two of you or a family night filled with games you know they enjoy. These special moments will remind your child how important they are to you, helping rebuild their confidence.

All isn't lost after a mistake! By following these steps, you can repair any damage to your relationship and develop an even deeper bond with your child.

Anjali and Nimisha's Story

Anjali often found herself losing her temper in public when her daughter Nimisha acted out. Anjali would snap at her on the spot, believing it was best to correct her behavior immediately. However, Anjali became concerned when she began to notice Nimisha becoming quieter and less outgoing. Normally, Anjali either ignored the tantrums completely or bribed Nimisha to stop, but these methods didn't bring any lasting change. Her approach wasn't working, and she knew it was time to find a different solution.

A few days later, Nimisha was having a particularly challenging day. While in the checkout line at the grocery store, she began to throw a tantrum over a candy bar. As Nimisha balled up her fists, screamed, and stomped her feet, Anjali felt the familiar surge of frustration. She was tempted to yell at Nimisha, but instead took a deep breath and calmly told her they would discuss it at home. Keeping her composure amidst the judgmental stares of other shoppers challenged Anjali, but with her goal in mind, she managed to hold back her usual impulse to scold. She finished checking out, calmly walked Nimisha to the car, and headed home.

Later, in the privacy of their living room, Anjali sat down with Nimisha and gently asked her why she was upset. Nimisha hesitated to tell her mother what was wrong, but after some coaxing, she eventually opened up. She admitted to feeling ignored when her mother was too busy to pay attention to her. Anjali listened attentively and validated Nimisha's feelings. After ensuring her daughter felt heard, Anjali explained why Nimisha's behavior in the store was unacceptable. They talked about better ways to express frustration and set up a plan for what to do the next time Nimisha felt overwhelmed.

Even though it was difficult at times, Anjali continued to use her new approach. Instead of reacting to tantrums with immediate anger, Anjali calmly reminded Nimisha that they would discuss the problem at home. This consistency helped Nimisha feel more secure and understood, and Anjali began to notice significant changes in her daughter's behavior. Nimisha became less prone to public outbursts, and better at communicating her needs. Best of all, thanks to her dedication, Anjali felt her relationship with Nimisha growing stronger and stronger. The struggle to change her initial reactions was tough for Anjali, but the improvement in Nimisha's behavior and their bond made it all worthwhile.

Quiet Time

Reflecting on the Past and Present

1. Think about a time when you were scolded in front of others as a child. How did it make you feel?

2. Did being scolded in public by your parents have the effect they hoped for? Or did it make things worse? Why do you think that is?

3. If you could go back, how would you ask your parents to handle those situations differently?

Practicing Private Discipline

1. Think of a recent time when you scolded your child in public. How did they react, and how did you feel afterward?

2. What steps can you take to make sure these conversations happen privately in the future? How will you remind yourself to handle it calmly?

3. When you've had private, respectful conversations with your child about their mistakes, what positive changes have you noticed in their behavior? Has it improved their confidence or how they respond?

Encouraging Respectful Communication

1. Can you think of situations where you could practice private discipline? What will you do differently to protect your child's dignity?

2. How can you use calm and respectful language to talk about your child's mistakes and guide them toward better choices? What phrases or tone can help keep the conversation constructive?

Activity: Calm Conversation Corner

Designate a private space for discussions about behavior and discipline, like a quiet corner in the house where you can talk without interruptions. To ensure you remain calm and respectful, practice deep breathing or a quick relaxation technique before addressing your child's behavior.

Self-Reminders for Parents

1. Personal Rule: Set a guideline like, "Always discuss serious matters in private." Repeat it to yourself throughout the day.
2. Visual Reminder: Place a small note that says, "Privacy for serious talks," throughout your home, car, office, or any other areas you frequent. You could also choose a symbol that represents this concept and place it on your note instead.
3. Alerts: Before anticipated discussions, use calendar reminders or phone alerts with messages like, "Discuss in private," to jog your memory.

Phrases to Initiate Private Conversations

- "Hey, can we talk about this somewhere private? It's important to me."
- "Let's step aside for a minute so we can chat without distractions."
- "I need to talk to you about something important. Can we find a quiet spot?"
- "This is a private matter. How about we go to your room or somewhere quiet to discuss it?"
- "I think we need to focus on this. Can we go somewhere quiet to talk?"

Final Thoughts

Your child is a person with their own feelings, emotions, and understanding of respect and kindness. They experience shame, embarrassment, and guilt just like you do, so treat them with the same kindness you'd want to be shown. At the same time, remember that they are still developing self-control—so give them all your guidance and support. Take a moment to rethink your role as a parent. Do you want to be remembered as just an enforcer of rules, or would you rather your little one look up to you as their most admired mentor and role model? Teach them how mistakes can be handled with grace and show them firsthand how to treat others with respect. When you embrace your parenting journey with love, support, and encouragement, you'll help your dear one grow into a responsible and empathetic person.

CHAPTER 5

Help Me Understand My Feelings

"Feelings are much like waves; we can't stop them from coming, but we can choose which one to surf." —Jonatan Mårtensson

Sometimes my feelings jumble up and get as tangled as my shoelaces! When you reassure me it's okay to feel my emotions—and teach me how to talk

about them- it's like handing me a flashlight to illuminate a dark room.

When you teach your child how to understand and manage their emotions, it's like granting them a superpower that lasts for life! This chapter explores the importance of helping kids develop the emotional intelligence that is crucial for their overall development and well-being. By teaching your child healthy ways to express and cope with their feelings, you prepare them to navigate life's hardest challenges.

Be My Emotional Compass

Imagine peeking inside your child's mind. Wouldn't it be great to know why they always fixate on the same pink crayon, hit their sibling for no reason, or constantly leave the fridge door open? Better yet, why do they sometimes seem to do the exact opposite of what they're told? When we're exhausted or frustrated, keeping our own emotions in check can sometimes feel like an uphill battle, making navigating our kids' emotions seem impossible. When your little one is upset, do you feel powerless and ignore their outbursts, hoping they'll get over it on their own? There are better ways to handle these moments. Let's talk about them.

First, consider your home environment. Is it comfortable and supportive or cold and chaotic? Home should be a safe place for kids to express their feelings without fear of being judged or dismissed. When your child is upset, avoid immediately asking questions like, *"Did you do something you shouldn't have?"* Instead of jumping to conclusions, try saying, *"I can see that you're upset right now. Let's talk about what's bothering you."* When you approach the situation in a stress-free way, you normalize your child's emotions, reassuring them that what they're feeling is valid and acceptable.

Be your child's emotional role model by handling your own feelings calmly and constructively. When you feel frustrated, express it clearly and show how you manage it: *"I'm feeling a bit frustrated because things didn't go as planned today. I'm going to calm myself down by taking a few deep breaths and taking a walk around the block."* Maturely handling your own emotions gives your child practical techniques for managing their own.

Help your little one identify and define their feelings. Phrases like, *"Don't be sad,"* can feel dismissive. Instead, try, *"It looks like you're feeling sad because your friend couldn't come over. I'm sure that's very disappointing. It's okay to feel what you're feeling."* Teaching your child to give a name to their emotions helps them better understand their feelings and communicate with them more effectively.

Help your child learn empathy by taking them for a walk in another person's shoes—encourage them to think about the feelings of others. For example, maybe your child is angry because a sibling accidentally broke their toy. Help them see the situation from another viewpoint by talking to them about how their sibling might feel about what happened—do they feel sadness, guilt, regret, or embarrassment about breaking the toy? Discuss and give a name to these emotions. Practice self-regulation techniques together, such as deep breathing or taking a break to calm down. By encouraging empathy and healthy stress-management techniques, you help your child learn to manage their emotions constructively, promoting emotional intelligence and resilience.

Child Brain Development

Understanding your child's brain development can be a game changer when it comes to effectively supporting their emotions. Early childhood is a time of rapid brain growth, especially in the regions of the brain that help regulate feelings and self-control. Knowing the science behind the behaviors can help you be more patient and supportive as your child learns and grows.

In young kids, the emotional part of the brain is very active, meaning they often have big reactions to small things and struggle to control their feelings. During difficult moments, remember that your child's brain is still learning how to process emotions. Instead of adding to the chaos by getting frustrated yourself, help them regulate—try comforting them and guiding them through their emotions. For example, if your child is upset because they don't want to get dressed, acknowledge their feelings and help them calm down.

As kids grow and mature, the part of the brain that regulates decision-making and self-control becomes better developed; this process continues through their teenage years. To support the brain's healthy growth, give your child plenty of chances to make decisions and solve problems, like giving them a hand in planning a family outing or letting them work out a disagreement with a friend. These opportunities help them learn to think critically about their actions and better manage their emotions.

To promote healthy brain development, focus on creating a supportive environment at home. Consistent routines, positive feedback, and open communication all help kids feel secure and understood. Activities like reading together, playing educational games, and engaging in creative play also boost brain growth. Your patience and support during these years build the foundation for your little one's emotional health and future success.

How to Model Healthy Emotional Responses

Children learn by watching us—especially when it comes to handling emotions, so be careful what lessons you're teaching! Our actions speak louder than words, and kids closely observe and mimic how we manage our feelings. When you regulate your own emotions in a healthy way, you teach your child valuable coping strategies.

- **Express Your Emotions Clearly**

If you're feeling overwhelmed, say so! By doing so, you normalize having feelings. You might say, *"I'm feeling a little stressed because I have a lot of errands I need to run. I think I'll take a few deep breaths to calm down."* This helps you manage your feelings and also shows your child how to express and attend to their own.

- **Use Constructive Language**

Avoid dismissive phrases like, *"It's not a big deal,"* or *"You'll get over it."* No one likes to have their feelings brushed off—so view the situation from your child's perspective, acknowledge its difficulty, and offer support. You could say, *"I see this is tough for you. Let's work through it together."* Validating their feelings and tackling problems together helps your child feel understood.

- **Demonstrate Calming Techniques**

Show your child how to use relaxation techniques when emotions run high. Doing activities like deep breathing, counting to ten, or taking a short walk together teaches them practical methods to manage their emotions—and helps you both unwind. Next time your youngster is upset, try saying, *"Let's calm down by taking three deep breaths together."*

- **Encourage Talking About Feelings**

Make discussing emotions part of your daily routine by asking your child about their feelings and talking about your own. Frequently asking questions like, *"How did that make you feel?"* fosters open communication and helps them feel more comfortable expressing their emotions.

- **Lead by Example**

If a child's environment is not supportive and uplifting, it's impossible to expect them to be calm and happy. When kids witness frequent yelling, arguing, and invalidation of emotions, they start to see these actions as the norm. Keep in mind the old adage, *"Monkey see, monkey do."* If you want your little one to manage their emotions, you have to model regulating your own. When you handle your feelings calmly, you teach them to do the same.

Kelsey and Mia's Story

Kelsey's daughter, Mia, often struggled with intense emotions when things didn't go her way. Kelsey was overwhelmed by Mia's tantrums, and she'd often bribe her daughter in a desperate attempt to stop them. Kelsey realized this approach was encouraging Mia's poor behavior by motivating her to act out to get what she wanted. Feeling frustrated and defeated, Kelsey began searching for a better solution.

One afternoon, Mia was upset because her tower of blocks had toppled over. She began to cry and scream. Kelsey kneeled down to Mia's level, made eye contact, and said, *"I can see you're upset that your tower fell. That must be so frustrating after all your hard work."*

Together, they took deep breaths, a calming technique Kelsey had carefully researched and practiced with Mia. After a few breaths, Mia's tears began to stop. By asking open-ended questions, Kelsey then encouraged Mia to talk about what happened and how she felt. Mia expressed her frustration and sadness, and Kelsey listened attentively, validating her daughter's emotions.

Next, Kelsey encouraged Mia to think about what they could do differently next time to make the tower stronger. They brainstormed ideas together, turning what started as a tantrum into a learning moment. Over time, with consistent practice and patience, Mia became better at expressing her emotions and finding constructive ways to deal with frustration. Kelsey noticed a significant improvement in Mia's ability to handle difficult situations, and they grew closer as they navigated these challenges together.

Quiet Time

Reflecting on the Past and Present

1. When you were a child, how did your parents respond when you were angry, sad, or upset? Did they listen and validate your feelings, or did they ignore them?

   _____
   _____
   _____

2. Think about how well you manage your emotions as an adult? Are there any areas where you could improve how you regulate your feelings?

3. Looking back, what do you wish your parents had done differently to help you handle your emotions better? How could that have changed the way you handle feelings now?

Understanding Feelings

1. Think of a recent time when your child was overwhelmed with emotions. How did you recognize what they were feeling, and what helped you understand them better?

2. What methods have you taught your child to help them recognize and express their emotions? Are these techniques working well for them? What could be improved?

3. How do you feel when your child is upset? Do you find yourself feeling calm, anxious, or something else?

Teaching Emotional Regulation

1. How do you manage your own emotions in front of your child? What do you think they learn from watching you handle difficult situations?

2. List a few strategies you can teach your child to help them handle emotions like anger or sadness. Are there any techniques you've found that work well?

3. Have you noticed your child picking up any unhelpful behaviors or phrases from you or your spouse? How did it make you feel, and what can you do differently to model positive behavior going forward?

Encouraging Expression

1. How often do you encourage your child to talk about their feelings? Think of a recent example where you supported them in expressing their emotions.

2. Can you recall a time when your child expressed their feelings in a positive way? How did you respond, and how can you continue to encourage this kind of behavior?

Activity: Emotional Wheel

What You'll Need:

- Paper
- Colored pencils, crayons, or markers

How to Do It:

The goal of this activity is to get your child to talk about their feelings. Create a wheel by drawing a large circle on a sheet of paper. Draw lines from the center (like slices of a pie or spokes of a wheel) and label each section with an emotion. For younger kids, focus on simple emotions like happy, sad, angry, or scared; for older children, include more nuanced emotions like frustration, content, and being overwhelmed. Color each section of the wheel.

Discuss each emotion on the wheel with your child and have them choose a section that matches their current mood. Next, to model empathy, share a related experience of your own. Use the wheel regularly, such as before bed or after a challenging event, to help your child learn to express their emotions. For a fun spin, create simple role-playing scenarios. For example, *"Imagine you lost your favorite toy at the park."* Ask your child which part of the wheel fits each feeling. Then discuss ways to handle those feelings.

Why It Helps:

This activity is a great way to give kids a visual representation of their emotions, helping them understand and share their feelings in an engaging way.

Sample Conversation:

- Parent: "I see you chose the 'angry' section. Can you tell me more about when you felt this way?"
- Child: "I felt angry when I couldn't find my favorite toy."
- Parent: "What do you think might help you feel better when you're angry?"

Phrases to Help Kids Handle Emotions

- "It's okay to feel upset; let's find a way to calm down together."
- "Use your words to tell me how you're feeling. I'm here to listen."
- "When you're feeling angry, take deep breaths to help yourself calm down. Let me show you how."

- "Let's list five things that cheer you up when you're feeling sad."
- "Feeling scared is normal; let's talk about what's bothering you."
- "It's okay to cry; tears can help us feel better sometimes."
- "When you're feeling frustrated, try taking a break and doing something you enjoy."
- "Remember, it's okay to ask for help when you're feeling overwhelmed."
- "Talking about your feelings can make them less scary."
- "Every emotion is valid, and it's important to express them in healthy ways."

Final Thoughts

Help your little one become an emotional superhero by teaching them to identify, express, and constructively manage their emotions! For your lesson to be effective, you have to talk the talk *and* walk the walk—manage your feelings in a healthy way so you can light the path for your little one. Journeying through the strong emotions common in youngsters can be a challenge, but the life skills your child will learn along the way make it well worth taking. As you walk this road together, you'll watch your child's emotional intelligence blossom and your bond strengthen.

CHAPTER 6

Your Apology Matters to Me

"An apology is the super glue of life. It can repair just about anything." —Lynn Johnston

If you accidentally forget to pick me up from soccer practice or miss my piano recital, please don't be too proud to say

sorry. Even if all you say is, "I'm sorry I couldn't make it today. I'll try my best to be there next time," your apology means the world to me.

Apologies can heal wounds, build trust, and teach valuable lessons about humility and responsibility. Why is saying sorry so important when you make a mistake that hurts your child? When you acknowledge your errors and apologize, you show your child that everyone makes mistakes—and that it's important to take responsibility for them. Apologizing when you need to—and meaning it—can fill your home with openness, trust, and mutual respect.

Saying Sorry the Right Way

"I may have messed up, but I don't really need to apologize because kids don't understand. They'll forget about what happened soon anyway." Sound familiar? If so, it's time to reframe your mindset. Just like all of us, children feel disappointed and disrespected when people don't apologize for their actions—it can be even more hurtful when this betrayal comes from their

parents. And apologizing isn't as simple as just saying the words, *"I'm sorry."* It's about sincerity—a genuine apology is a powerful tool that teaches children about accountability, empathy, and the importance of making things right.

Think back to a time when a loved one made a mistake that hurt you. Did they apologize? If so—and if the apology was sincere—you probably appreciated that they valued your feelings enough to try to fix things. If they didn't apologize, or if all they gave was a forced and rushed *"sorry,"* you were likely left feeling hurt, dismissed, or even angry. If you neglect to apologize to your child, they feel the same hurt. When you genuinely apologize for a mistake, like accidentally breaking a toy or losing your temper, you show them humility and respect. Parroting the word *"sorry"* without any feeling behind it is not enough; you must truly mean it.

As a parent, you are the moon and the stars to your little one; they look up to you as their biggest role model. When they see you admitting your faults, they learn that mistakes are part of life—and that what truly matters is how you handle and grow from them. When you sincerely apologize, you teach your child honesty and accountability, repair broken trust, and take your communication and understanding to a deeper level.

Let's say you had to miss your child's basketball game because of an urgent work meeting. A heartfelt apology and a promise to change can go a long way to making them feel better. Saying, *"I'm sorry I couldn't make it—I know how important it was to you. I rescheduled Friday's meeting so I can come to your next game!"* shows you care about their feelings and are committed to making things right.

Witnessing a true apology also builds emotional intelligence in children by encouraging them to express their own feelings and empathize with others. When they see you making an effort to right a wrong, they think harder about the impact their actions have on others; this is the foundation of empathy.

Making sincere apologies part of the family culture is one of the best ways to create an environment of confidence, tolerance, and security. When your child understands you're on their team, you'll be able to tackle any conflict or misunderstanding that life throws your way. Next time you make a mistake, remember that a genuine apology, filled with sincerity and understanding, can make a world of difference to your child.

Laura and Mia's story

Meet Laura and her daughter, Mia. Because of her upbringing, Laura had always believed that apologizing to children wasn't necessary. She didn't think kids would remember or truly understand mistakes that hurt them. She often dismissed Mia's feelings, and when she did apologize, she opted for a quick and empty *"sorry."*

One Saturday, Laura promised to take Mia to the park after catching up on some work emails. Laura sat down at her computer, and she lost track of time. When Mia eagerly reminded her of their plans, Laura brushed her off with a quick, *"Sorry, maybe next time,"* barely even looking up from her laptop. Mia's excited smile faded, but, too busy with her work, Laura didn't notice.

That evening, Mia barely said a word during dinner. Confused and concerned, Laura asked her what was wrong. With tears in her eyes, Mia said, *"You always say we'll go to the park, but we never do. I feel like you don't care about spending time with me."* Laura's first instinct was to react defensively, but she saw the pain in Mia's eyes. She hadn't given her casual dismissals a second thought, but it was clear they were hurting her daughter.

After Mia went to bed, Laura reflected on how she often put other priorities before her daughter. Determined to make things right, she decided to genuinely address her mistakes and change. The next morning, she sat down with Mia and apologized sincerely. *"Mia, I'm sorry I didn't take you to the park yesterday,"* she began. *"I know I've done this before, and it's not fair to you. I promise I'll do better, and I'm truly sorry for letting you down. I'd love to take you to the park today, let's go get dressed!"* Mia was surprised and cautious, but she saw the sincerity in her mother's eyes. She nodded, accepting the apology with a hopeful smile.

From then on, Laura made a conscious effort to follow through on her promises and to truly apologize whenever she slipped up. With her busy schedule and habit of brushing off her obligations, this wasn't always easy. To help keep herself on the right track, she began setting reminders and actively planning activities with Mia to show she valued their time together. With consistency and commitment to keeping her word, she established an open and trusting relationship with her daughter.

☺ Encouraging Your Child to Apologize

Just like you, your child can learn how to say, *"I'm sorry,"* when they've done something wrong. A good foundation for encouraging this is by modeling sincere apologies of your own. When your child sees you putting trying to make things right, they learn that it's important for them to do the same.

Imagine your child accidentally breaking a friend's toy. Instead of scolding them, you can gently say, *"I know it was an accident, but it would be kind to apologize to your friend. Saying 'I'm sorry' shows that you care about their feelings."*

Make sure to explain that the words *"I'm sorry"* aren't the most important part of an apology—it's about really meaning it.

By making genuine apologies of your own and encouraging your child to do the same, you help them grow into a thoughtful and caring person. This is a skill that will ensure they are kind and responsible in all their relationships.

Quiet Time

Reflecting on the Past and Present

1. When you were a child, how did your parents handle their mistakes? Did they apologize, or did they move on without addressing them?

2. Do you believe it's important for parents to apologize to their children? Why or why not?

Learning from Apologies

1. Think about the last time you apologized to your child. What was the situation? How did you apologize, and how did your child respond?

2. What did you and your child learn from this experience about mistakes and forgiveness? Did it bring you closer or help your child understand something new?

Addressing Skipped Apologies

1. Think of a time you made a mistake but didn't apologize to your child. Maybe you missed an event or said something unkind. How could an apology have helped in that moment?

2. What can you do now to make up for a time you didn't apologize? Is there a way to repair the relationship and show your child you're sorry?

Activity: Apology Role-Playing

Scenario 1: Missed Event

- **Situation**: You promised to attend your child's school play but missed it due to an emergency at work.
- **Your Reactions**: How did you feel when you realized you missed the play? How do you think your child felt?
- **Phrase to Try**: *"I'm really sorry for missing your play tonight. I know it was important to you, and I wanted to be there. Let's pick a special day this weekend to spend together, just the two of us. What would you like to do?"*

Scenario 2: False Accusation

- **Situation**: You scolded your child for breaking a vase but later discovered that the dog did it.

- **Your Reactions**: How did you react when you found out your child didn't break the vase? How did your child feel about being wrongly accused?
- **Phrase to Try**: *"I owe you an apology. I found out it wasn't you who broke the vase, and I'm sorry for accusing you. I should have asked you instead of assuming; I promise to put more trust in you next time. Thank you for being understanding."*

Scenario 3: Overreaction

- **Situation**: You overreacted and raised your voice when your child failed to do their homework on time.
- **Your Reactions**: What led to your overreaction about the homework? How did your child feel after the incident?
- **Phrase to Try**: *"I'm sorry for getting so upset about your homework. It's important, but I shouldn't have yelled. Let's work out a schedule together so things feel less overwhelming. What do you think about us checking your homework plan every Sunday evening?"*

❖ Family Apology Templates

- "I'm sorry for [specific action]. I understand it upset you. How can I help us move forward?"
- "I made a mistake by [specific action]. I'm really sorry. Let's talk about how to make things right."
- "I apologize for [specific action]. It wasn't my intention to hurt you. Can you tell me how you're feeling?"
- "I realize now that I was wrong to [specific action]. I'm sorry for the pain I caused. What can I do to make it up to you?"
- "I'm sorry for not understanding your feelings earlier. I want to learn and improve. Can we discuss this more?"

- "I regret [specific action] and how it hurt you. I'm committed to doing better. Can we work on this together?"
- "I'm sorry for missing out on [specific event or action]. I want you to know how much I care about you. Can we plan another activity to do together?"
- "I owe you an apology for [specific action]. It was not right. I want to listen to you and figure out how to change."

Final Thoughts

A heartfelt apology is like a magic spell that builds trust and shows your little one that everyone makes mistakes; what matters is how we learn from them. A sincere "I'm sorry" and a promise to change can make a world of difference to a hurting child, all while teaching them the value of humility and compassion.

CHAPTER 7

Teach Me Gently

"Peace is not the absence of conflict, but the ability to handle conflict by peaceful means." —Ronald Reagan

Physical punishment hurts and confuses me. I'm trying my best to be good, really! Please use words instead of your hands to work things out. When you talk to me

gently, it's like a hug for my ears, helping me learn without any ouchies.

Everyone knows that hitting hurts, but the pain it can cause is way more than skin deep; this kind of punishment breaks kids' trust, making them confused and scared. In this chapter, we will learn all about the dangers of physical punishment and how to compassionately discipline without it. By using positive reinforcement and focusing on communication, you'll create a home environment that supports your child's emotional well-being, naturally promoting healthy behavior.

Rethinking Discipline

Do you often find yourself reacting with the urge to hit when your child crosses a line or makes a mistake? It's time to rethink this approach. Let's recall Aesop's fable *The North Wind and the Sun*. The North Wind and the Sun compete to get a traveler to remove his coat. The North Wind's forceful attempts at blasting the traveler's coat off with icy gusts only make him hold onto it more tightly. The Sun, however, chooses a peaceful method, shining down on the traveler with warm rays. The traveler feels comfortable enough to open up and immediately takes off his coat. We can learn a lot from this story about discipline; a gentle approach is often more effective than force.

Force might stop unwanted behavior briefly because of the fear and pain it causes. But it doesn't address the root cause or teach why the behavior was wrong. Instead of improving behavior in the long run, it causes fear, confusion, and resentment. Over time, kids who are physically punished can develop anxiety, depression, and even aggressive behavior.

Think about it from an adult perspective: What if your boss slammed his hands on the desk in anger because you made a mistake at work? It's unlikely you'd feel sorry for what you did; you'd probably just feel frustrated and disturbed by the outburst. Children feel the same way when confronted with aggressive behavior.

It can be tough to reframe your mindset if you were raised in a home where physical punishment was the norm, but there are better alternatives that can make your home a more peaceful and orderly place. Clear and civil communication is one of these. Instead of hitting, use words to explain why a behavior is unacceptable and talk to your child about how to better cope with what they're feeling. This gently helps them understand consequences and boosts their ability to manage their emotions. Positive reinforcement, such as praising your little one when they follow the rules, is also a great way to encourage good behavior. The goal is to teach your child they are loved and respected, even when they make mistakes.

Show your child that lessons can be learned without pain or fear, and you'll watch them blossom as they learn valuable life skills. Your whole family will enjoy the peace and comfort of a home free from intimidation or force. Think differently, discipline differently. Your precious one deserves it.

Are You Missing Teachable Moments?

When you're angry, it's easy to get tunnel vision and miss valuable teachable moments that can help your child grow. Rage can cloud your judgment, blinding you to the opportunities to explain, guide, and teach.

Imagine your child spilling grape juice on the carpet. In the heat of the moment, your instinct may be to yell and reach out to hit them. But if you take a deep breath, calm down, and identify the teachable moment, you'll realize this slip-up is an opportunity to explain why it's important to be careful with drinks. Next, you can involve them in cleaning up the mess. You've just turned a frustrating mishap into a lesson on caution, responsibility, and consequences. And you did it all without fear or pain!

When your child makes a mistake and you're tempted to lash out, flip the script, instead use the chance to unlock a teachable moment. You need to have a level head for a teachable moment to be effective, so first take a second to calm yourself down. Then, explain why your child's behavior is unacceptable and discuss better choices for the future. This helps them learn from their mistakes, making them less likely to repeat the same behavior.

Next time you feel anger bubbling up, pause. Ask yourself if there's a teachable moment hidden under the surface. By focusing on education rather than punishment, you create a supportive environment where your child can grow and learn. Embrace these moments—they are opportunities to build trust and understanding. You'll be amazed as you watch your child's behavior improve over time.

Tim used to believe that physical punishment was necessary for raising kids. He was raised in a household where hitting was the norm; his parents often spanked him when he did something wrong. Tim took the same approach with his own kids, believing he was doing the right thing by showing them *"tough love."* Something felt wrong about the fear in their eyes when they knew a punishment was coming, though, and Tim began to reflect on his own childhood.

He thought back to how he felt after his parents physically punished him: Did the spankings truly help him recognize and correct his mistakes, or did they just make him resentful and rebellious? All he could remember was fear, anger, and injustice. If he could go back in time, would he want his parents to discipline him with a harsh hand, or would he rather they talk to him gently and explain his mistakes?

Thinking about these questions, Tim decided to change his approach with his kids. He learned that physical punishment often stems from parents' frustration and emotional reactions rather than a desire to teach. This is far from being a teachable moment. This concept he learned is crucial in effective parenting.

One day, his daughter accidentally broke a vase. Instead of reacting with anger, Tim took a deep breath and had a calm conversation with her. They talked about why the vase was important and how to avoid such accidents in the future. Then Tim involved her in cleaning up the mess. This helped his daughter understand her mistake and the consequences without feeling scared or resentful.

Over time, Tim noticed the atmosphere of their home becoming lighter. His children began to open up more, sharing their thoughts and feelings without fear, bringing them all closer. By focusing on teachable moments and clear communication, Tim built trust and mutual respect that improved his children's behavior.

Quiet Time

Reflecting on the Past and Present

1. Did your parents use physical punishment when you were growing up? How did it make you feel at the time? Was it necessary?

   _____
   _____
   _____

2. How has your experience with physical punishment during childhood shaped how you discipline your own children? Do you notice any similarities or differences?

3. Do you find yourself reacting physically when your child misbehaves? What tends to trigger this response, and how do you feel about it?

Understanding the Impact

1. What emotional or psychological effects do you think physical punishment might have on your child? How might it influence their behavior or attitude in the long run?

2. Have you noticed changes in your child's behavior that could be linked to physical punishment? If so, what are those changes?

3. How does your child respond when you use positive reinforcement instead of physical punishment? What differences do you see in their behavior?

4. List a few alternative strategies you could use instead of physical punishment. How could you apply these in future situations?

Promoting Positive Behavior

1. Identify three positive reinforcement techniques you can use to encourage good behavior in your child.

2. How can you model non-physical discipline techniques to teach your child how to handle conflicts or frustrations? What are some examples you can use?

Recognizing Teachable Moments

1. Think of a recent time when your child misbehaved. Did you take the opportunity to explain why the behavior was wrong? How did you handle it?

2. How often do you miss teachable moments because of emotional or impulsive reactions? How can you change this pattern and be more mindful?

3. Reflect on a teachable moment you handled well. What did you do, and how did your child respond? How can you use this approach more often?

activity: Plan for Positivity

> **Step 1: Identify Frustrating Scenarios**

Think about situations that often lead to frustration or conflict in your home, causing you to feel tempted to react physically. Write down three or four of these common scenarios.

For example:

- Scenario 1: Your child spills juice on the carpet after being told to be careful.
- Scenario 2: Sibling arguments escalate into pushing or hitting.
- Scenario 3: Your child refuses to get dressed for school.

➤ Step 2: Write Down Your Triggers

For each scenario, think about what specifically triggers your frustration and write it down. Understanding these triggers will help you manage your reactions more effectively.

For example:

- Scenario 1 Trigger: Feeling frustrated because of the mess and extra work.
- Scenario 2 Trigger: Worrying about injuries and arguments.
- Scenario 3 Trigger: Stress from being rushed in the morning.

➤ Step 3: Plan Positive Responses

Now, for each scenario, brainstorm and write down two positive, non-physical ways you can respond to the situation. Focus on calm, constructive actions that teach your child without causing fear.

For example:

- Scenario 1 Positive Response: Take a deep breath, explain calmly why spills happen, and involve your child in the cleanup. Use the moment to teach about being careful and praise their help in cleaning up.
- Scenario 2 Positive Response: Separate the siblings, give them a moment to calm down, and then talk through the conflict with them. Introduce a "cool down" period and discuss how to express feelings without hitting.
- Scenario 3 Positive Response: Offer your child choices, like picking between two outfits, to give them a sense of control. Use positive reinforcement by praising them when they follow instructions quickly.

> **Step 4: Implement and Reflect**

Over the next week, practice these positive responses when frustrating scenarios arise. At the end of the week, take a moment to reflect on how things went. Did you notice any changes in your child's behavior or your reactions? Write down your observations to track your progress.

Gentle Reminders: Kind Hands, Kind Words

- "Hands are for helping, not hurting."
- "Let's use our words to express feelings, not our hands."
- "It's important to treat everyone with kindness and respect."
- "We solve problems by talking, not hitting."
- "Everyone deserves to feel safe and loved."
- "If you're upset, take a deep breath and explain what's bothering you."
- "Hitting hurts others and doesn't solve problems."
- "I understand you're angry, but we don't use our hands to show it."
- "Let's find a calm way to discuss what's upsetting you."
- "We show love and respect by keeping our hands to ourselves."

Final Thoughts

It can be challenging to reframe a mindset you've held since childhood, but you owe it to your little one. By trading physical punishment for consistent, fair, and gentle discipline, you teach respect and responsibility. Leaving force and intimidation in the past where they belong will help your child grow into the best adult they can be.

CHAPTER 8

No Yelling Zone

"Raise your words, not your voice. It is rain that grows flowers, not thunder." –Rumi

Yelling scares me and makes me feel lost. It's like thunder inside the house, and I don't know where to hide. I'm trying really, really hard to listen and be good—I promise. Please use gentle words; they

help me understand and learn without fear.

Think yelling is the best way to grab your child's attention quickly? Think again! In this chapter, we will discuss the negative effects of yelling on kids—and why it's so important to use calm and gentle communication instead. Yelling causes fear and confusion which leads to stress and bad behavior. By focusing on relaxed and positive communication instead, you can create a supportive and peaceful home environment.

Avoiding Frustration

Power struggles: They're no fun for any of us. If you often find yourself raising your voice in frustration because your child resists your instructions or requests, try involving them by giving a few options to choose from. This empowers your child and gives them a sense of control, making them more likely to cooperate.

Here's what it looks like: Let's say you're getting your little one dressed for school. Convincing them to put on their jacket before heading out the door often results in resistance and frustration. Today, instead of demanding they wear their jacket, you try asking, *"Do you want to wear the blue jacket or the red jacket today?"* With just a simple question, you shift the focus from compliance or refusal to decision-making, allowing your child to feel involved and respected.

Keep the choices simple and positive (and ensure they're all outcomes you are happy with!). If it's time to clean up toys, instead of saying, *"Clean up your toys now,"* try, *"Would you like to put away the blocks first or the cars?"* This way, your child has a sense of control, making the task seem more manageable and less demanding.

Like most things, you'll find consistency is the key to this tactic. Regularly offering choices helps children understand that cooperation leads to rewarding outcomes. You can easily fit this method into your daily routine. For example, each morning, you can offer, *"Do you want to get dressed or brush your teeth first?"* If you keep at it, your child will start to anticipate this pattern and respond more readily. Over time, they will learn that listening and following instructions can be a positive experience rather than a negative one.

How to Connect with Your Child

Kids are more likely to listen when they feel connected with and loved by their parents. When your youngster feels a strong bond with you, they cooperate and follow instructions more easily meaning you'll feel less of a need to yell. But remember: Don't expect your child to bridge the gap; as a parent, it's your responsibility to connect with them.

Building a strong, trusting relationship with your child sets the stage for their emotional and psychological well-being. Here are some practical strategies to deepen your connection:

☺ Start the Day with Warmth

Mornings set the tone for the entire day, so make them a positive start! Waking up to a warm smile and a sunny greeting can start the day right by making your child feel loved and secure. A gentle hug, a loving smile, and a phrase like, *"Good morning, sunshine! Ready for a great day?"* can lift their mood and brighten their whole day!

☺ Involve, Encourage, and Appreciate

It might surprise you, but a great way to reinforce your child's importance to the family is by involving them in daily chores. This helps remind them that their contributions are a big deal—it also teaches them responsibility. When your little one helps set the table or cleans up their toys, acknowledge their effort with an enthusiastic, *"I really appreciate your help—you did a fantastic job!"* When you shower them with praise, it shows them you notice and value their efforts. By involving your child in age-appropriate tasks, you also instill a sense of accomplishment and teamwork.

☺ Communicate with Kindness

Discipline is a necessary part of parenting, but how you do it matters. Instead of using harsh words, speak with a firm yet kind tone and explain the reasons behind the rules. If you catch your little one scribbling on the wall, calmly say, *"We draw on paper, not on walls. Drawing on the walls can damage our home, and then we have to spend our free time cleaning instead of playing. Let's clean this up together and find some paper for your artwork."* When you explain calmly instead of yelling, you help them understand the lesson without feeling hurt or confused. This approach also teaches respect and accountability.

☺ Make Mealtimes Memorable

Mealtimes are a great opportunity to bond with your child. Get rid of distractions like the TV and phones, and use these moments to share stories, discuss your day, and listen to your child's experiences. Ask open-ended questions like, *"What was the best part of your day?"* or *"Did anything funny happen at school?"* Make family mealtimes a priority to build a sense of togetherness and strengthen your family bond. You'll encourage open communication and create memories to last a lifetime.

☺ Start and End on an Uplifting Note

Start the school day with a positive send-off! A smile and a hug can give your child the motivation they need to face the day. Say something encouraging like, *"You're going to do great today—I can't wait to hear all about it!"* When the school day is over, greet your child warmly to remind them that they belong. A cheerful, *"Welcome back! Tell me all about your day!"* shows that you truly care about their experiences and feelings.

☺ Create Calming Bedtime Routines

End the day on a happy note with a soothing bedtime routine. Read a story, have a quiet talk, or simply enjoy a cuddle together. Make bedtime a moment your child looks forward to by letting them choose a relaxing activity: *"Would you like to read a book together or talk about our favorite parts of the day before you sleep? I can't wait to unwind with you!"* These routines make bedtime a cherished and peaceful part of the day, providing comfort and a sense of security as your sweetie drifts off to sleep.

Lisa and Emma's Story

Lisa often found herself yelling when her energetic daughter Emma didn't listen. Their mornings were chaotic, filled with resistance, tears, and frustration. One tough morning, Emma threw a tantrum over getting dressed. Lisa shouted in anger above the screams, and Emma cried even louder. Feeling defeated and desperate, Lisa knew this wasn't sustainable. Something had to change.

That day Lisa confided in a friend about her struggles. She suggested a strategy that had worked for her children: the concept of giving choices. Lisa wondered if something so simple could really make a difference, but she decided she had nothing to lose by giving it a try. The next morning, instead of commanding Emma to get ready, Lisa gently offered a choice. *"Would you like to brush your teeth before or after you get dressed?"* she asked. Emma, who usually fought every step of the morning routine, looked surprised. She paused for a moment and then chose to brush her teeth first.

To Lisa's amazement, this small change made the morning run much smoother. Emma felt empowered by having a say in her routine, and Lisa noticed an immediate reduction in resistance. Encouraged by this success, Lisa began incorporating choices into other parts of their day. Instead of demanding, *"Pick up your toys now,"* she asked, *"Do you want to pick up the blocks first or the stuffed animals?"* Gradually, Emma started responding more positively to requests, and the power struggles that once ruled their lives began to fade. Lisa couldn't believe it when she noticed she'd gone an entire week without raising her voice at her daughter!

It wasn't an instant fix, and there were days when old habits crept back in. Lisa had to remind herself to stay calm and offer choices. With consistency and patience, their home went from chaotic to peaceful. Emma became more cooperative and adaptable, and the reduced frustration allowed Lisa to feel a stronger connection with her daughter. The mornings, once a battleground, became a smooth routine full of teamwork and shared smiles.

Sometimes the key to better communication and reduced stress is as simple as giving a choice. This small change helped Lisa manage her frustration and empowered her child to make decisions, creating an environment of harmony and respect.

Quiet Time

Reflecting on the Past and Present

1. What did your parents commonly get angry about when you were a child? How often did they raise their voices?

2. Did their yelling ever make you feel like you were a bad child? How did it impact your self-esteem?

3. Was there anything about your parents' discipline that you appreciated or understood, despite their anger?

4. How did you wish your parents had handled their anger instead? Looking back, do you think their reactions were reasonable?

5. What influence do you think your childhood experiences have had on your patience as a parent? Do you notice similarities in how you react to frustration?

Identifying Triggers and Managing Reactions

1. What are the common situations that lead you to raise your voice at your child? How do these situations affect you emotionally and physically?

2. How can you manage your reactions differently in the heat of the moment? Think of specific strategies you can use to stay calm.

3. Recall a recent time when you yelled at your child. How did they react immediately and afterward? How did you feel, and what would you like to change next time?

Developing Calm Responses

1. Create a plan for how you can respond calmly when you're tempted to yell. This could include deep breaths, taking a pause, or practicing positive self-talk.

2. How can you use positive reinforcement to encourage good behavior in your child? What's one technique you can start using today?

3. What methods can you teach your child to handle conflicts and frustrations without yelling? How can you model these behaviors?

Activity: Practicing "I" Statements

It can be easy to fall into the habit of blaming your kids with phrases like, *"You upset me again," "You're making me crazy,"* or, *"You're out of control."* Instead of playing the blame game, focus on stating how you feel and what you want. "I" statements reduce conflict by helping you communicate your emotions clearly and effectively without putting your child on the defensive.

Keeping a journal can be a great way to track your progress as you practice "I" statements. Each time you successfully use an "I" statement, jot it down. Reflect on the situation, how you handled it, and how your child responded. Over time, this journal will help you see patterns, recognize your growth, and identify areas where you can improve. It's a great way to stay motivated and mindful as you work towards creating a more peaceful home.

Here are some examples to help you practice:

- **Situation 1**: Your child leaves their toys scattered all over the floor.
    - **Typical Reaction**: "Why do you always make such a mess? You never clean up after yourself!"
    - **Improved Response**: *"I feel frustrated when the toys are left out because I want our home to be tidy."*

- **Situation 2**: Your child doesn't listen when you ask them to do something.
    - **Typical Reaction**: "You never listen to me! Do as I say right now!"
    - **Improved Response**: *"I feel upset when I have to repeat myself because it makes me feel ignored."*

- **Situation 3**: Your child is arguing with their sibling.
    - **Typical Reaction**: "Stop fighting! You two are driving me insane!"
    - **Improved Response**: *"I feel frustrated when you two argue because I want you to get along and be happy."*

- **Situation 4**: Your child refuses to eat the meal you prepared.
    - **Typical Reaction**: "You're so picky! Why can't you just eat what's on your plate?"
    - **Improved Response**: *"I feel disappointed when you don't eat the meal I made because I want you to grow strong and be healthy."*

- **Situation 5**: Your child is taking too long to get ready in the morning.
  - **Typical Reaction**: "Hurry up! We're going to be late because of you!"
  - **Improved Response**: *"I feel stressed when we're running late because I want us to be on time."*

Note: "I" statements usually help reduce defensiveness and promote clear communication, but every child is different—some kids might be distressed by direct language. If your child reacts negatively, you can first offer physical comfort like a tight hug to provide immediate reassurance and help them feel safe. Then be flexible and adapt your approach based on your child's individual needs and responses.

Self-Reminders for Parents to Prevent Yelling

- "I will speak softly to set a good example."
- "Let me listen more and raise my voice less."
- "Staying calm will help me understand and be understood."
- "Yelling doesn't solve problems; patience and words do."
- "I choose to express my feelings without shouting."
- "My calm voice can create a peaceful home."
- "Before speaking, I will take a deep breath."
- "I'm here to guide, not intimidate. Let's solve this together."
- "Using a gentle tone fosters trust and respect."
- "By staying calm, I can teach my child how to handle stress."

Final Thoughts

Transitioning to a no-yelling parenting style won't happen overnight; it takes time and effort. But with mindfulness, determination, and a focus on respectful communication, you can build a strong, loving connection with your child. Understand your triggers, practice calm responses, and use "I" statements to communicate clearly. With practice and patience, you can make your home a safe space free from unkind and intimidating words.

CHAPTER 9

Peel Off the Labels

"Labels are for jars, not people." —Unknown

When you label me "shy," "picky eater," or "difficult kid," it makes me feel like I can't change or grow. I want to be seen for all the cool things I can do, so please don't put limits on my potential. Let's discover my strengths together, without any labels holding us back.

When you label your child, you create a sticky trap that locks them into that identity. In this chapter, we'll talk about why it's so important to avoid labels and instead focus on celebrating your little one's individuality. Labels can limit kids' self-perception and hinder their growth. Let's learn about how emphasizing their strengths and positive traits instead can help them build a healthy self-image.

Choose Your Words Wisely

Your words have power! If you label your child as "selfish," "lazy," or "frustrating," those descriptors can become ingrained in their minds, trapping them within those negative identities. This power works both ways: Being labeled an "angry parent" might make you see yourself that way but being recognized for your understanding or compassion can reinforce those traits. Words don't just float away after you say them—they can take root and sprout. Using positive, encouraging language can help your child grow into a confident individual, while negative labels can lead to low self-esteem and self-doubt.

When you label your child, you shape how they see themselves—even if you don't mean to. Pay attention to the nicknames you give your little one as well. Even well-intended nicknames that parents view as cute can be hurtful to children, harming their self-esteem and sparking negative self-talk. Lovingly referring to your child as "scaredy-cat" or "crybaby" might seem harmless, but nicknames like these can cause the same problems as labels. Labels and nicknames can create self-fulfilling prophecies where kids start to believe and act according to them.

Let's consider an adult perspective. In the workplace, if you are labeled as a successful hard worker, you'll likely feel motivated to keep up the good performance. But if you're labeled as slow or unreliable, you might lose motivation altogether, thinking, *"Everyone already knows I'm slow, so why bother?"* Labels can assign fixed identities, creating expectations and pressures and shaping behavior in powerful ways. Children share the same tendency to act according to labels, and the effects can last a lifetime.

It's important to remember that your child is constantly growing, learning, and evolving. By focusing on their strengths and all the wonderful things that make them unique, you can encourage their growth and development. Instead of labeling, let's celebrate what makes them special and explore their full potential alongside them.

Watch Out for Unintentional Labels

Did you know that, sometimes, even positive labels like "smart" or "talented" can create anxiety for your child? While these labels might seem like compliments, they can make your child feel pressured to always live up to that expectation. For example, if your child is always called "the smart one," they might avoid trying new things because they fear they might fail and end up disappointing you or themselves.

To avoid this, shift from praising fixed traits to praising the effort and progress your child makes. Instead of saying, *"You're so smart,"* you could say, *"I'm proud of how hard you worked on that project."* This helps your child understand that it's okay to try new things, make mistakes, and grow from the experience. Encouraging a growth mindset teaches them that abilities can be developed with effort and time, helping them feel confident in exploring new challenges.

The key is being mindful of the words you use; you can support your child's growth without unintentionally limiting them to a specific label. Use your support to help them unlock and explore their full potential!

Maria and Alex's Story

Maria faced a tough situation with her son Alex, who was being labeled as the "troublemaker" at school. Every meeting with his teachers seemed to center around his bad behavior. As time passed, Alex started to internalize this label, acting out more frequently because he believed it was expected of him.

One day, Maria attended a parent-teacher conference and was flooded with complaints about Alex's behavior, leaving her frustrated and helpless. That evening, she noticed Alex sulking in his room. Maria quietly walked in, sat down next to him, and placed her hand on his shoulder. *"Some of those things must have been difficult for you to hear,"* she said softly. *"Can we talk about what you're feeling now?"* Alex leaned in and confessed that he felt everyone saw him as a troublemaker. He embraced the label and acted the part since he believed it was too late to change their minds. Maria finally realized the negative impact this label was having on her son, and she decided to take action.

She started by addressing the issue with his teachers, asking them to recognize and praise Alex's positive qualities instead of solely focusing on his wrongdoings. This was not an easy task—old habits die hard—and it took several discussions to shift the teachers' mindsets. At home, Maria faced her own struggles. It was challenging to break the cycle of constantly scolding Alex, but she made a conscious effort to celebrate his efforts and progress, no matter how small. Maria used specific praise like, *"I noticed how hard you worked on your homework today—great job!"* and *"Thank you for helping set the table; that was very thoughtful."*

There were days when Alex would go back to his old behaviors, and Maria felt like giving up. But she kept working, knowing that change wouldn't happen overnight. Slowly but surely, Alex's behavior began to improve. He started to see himself in a more positive light, realizing he didn't have to live up to the "troublemaker" label.

The journey wasn't easy, but Maria changed the narrative by focusing on Alex's positive attributes rather than his misbehavior. In doing so, she helped her son develop a healthier self-image and more positive behavior patterns, transforming his self-perception and outlook on life.

Quiet Time

Reflecting on the Past and Present

1. Were you given any labels as a child by your parents, siblings, or others? How did those labels make you feel?

2. Did the labels you were given affect your confidence and behavior? In what ways?

Understanding Labels

1. Think about any nicknames or labels you use for your child. How might those words make them feel?

2. Talk to your child about how they feel regarding any labels or nicknames they've been given. How do they feel about them?

3. What positive words can you use to describe your child to help them feel good about themselves? How can you focus on their strengths?

Focusing on the Good

1. List three things your child is good at. How can you remind them of these every day?

2. How can you regularly praise your child's positive traits and achievements? What can you do to make this a daily habit?

3. What steps can you take to help your child see and celebrate their own strengths?

Helping Them Grow

1. Think of a time your child did something special. How did you respond, and what did it reveal about their potential?

2. Ask your child about their goals and interests. How can you work together to support these dreams?

3. How can you give your child opportunities to explore and grow their interests and talents?

activity: "My Strengths Collage"

What You'll Need:

- A poster board or large piece of paper
- Magazines, newspapers, or printed pictures
- Scissors
- Glue
- Markers
- Photos of your child
- Stickers

How to Do It:

Talk about what makes your child special, the things they're good at, and the activities they enjoy. Look through magazines or newspapers to find pictures and words that describe these traits. Cut them out together. Help your child glue the cutouts onto the poster board or paper. Encourage them to decorate the collage further with drawings, stickers, and photos of themselves. Place the collage somewhere your child can see it every day, like in their room or on the refrigerator.

Why It's Helpful:

This activity builds confidence—seeing their strengths every day gives your child a self-esteem boost and reminds them of all the things that make them special.

☺ Spotlight Your Child's Strengths

- "Focus on the light, not the shadows."
- "Look for the gold, not the dirt."
- "See the potential; nurture the growth."
- "Celebrate the small victories—they lead to big dreams."
- "Behind every behavior is a feeling. Try to understand it."
- "Children bloom with sunshine, not with thunder."
- "Emphasize the positives, and the challenges will shrink."
- "Your child's story is still being written. See the big picture, not just the page."
- "Every child shines differently—find what makes yours sparkle."

Final Thoughts

Words can be tools to build confidence or weapons to tear it down. How will you use yours? By avoiding labels and celebrating your youngster's unique qualities, you can help them grow into a confident and self-respecting person. Treat your child with the dignity they deserve by concentrating on the strengths and special traits that make them who they are. Choose to focus on the positive, and you'll encourage your little one to become their best self, free from the stickiness of limiting labels.

CHAPTER 10

Help Me Follow the Rules

"Boundaries are a part of self-care. They are healthy, normal, and necessary." —Doreen Virtue

I need fair rules to teach me what's right and wrong—they make me feel safe, stable and cared for. Please show me the

way! When you do, it's like having a map that leads me to the best version of myself.

Just like traffic signs guide us and prevent accidents as we drive, clear rules and boundaries help children explore their world safely and confidently. In this chapter, you'll learn how to set practical and effective rules that meet your child's real-world needs. Fair boundaries will nurture their sense of security and self-discipline and make your home a more peaceful place for the whole family.

Why Boundaries Matter

Imagine a playground with no fence. It's surrounded by busy roads—dangers could come from any angle at any time. Both kids and caregivers are so on edge they're barely even able to concentrate on having fun! Rules are like a fence around a playground; they protect kids from harm, making their home a safe place where they can focus on enjoying themselves.

In this section, you'll learn all about setting effective boundaries and helping your child follow them but remember: Don't be surprised if they test the limits. While it can be frustrating, this behavior is normal and necessary for healthy development. Setting clear rules and explaining the "why" behind them can help your child understand that boundaries exist for a reason, making them more likely to cooperate.

How Differing Parenting Styles Confuse Kids

We all have different backgrounds, different viewpoints, and different expectations. That means parents often have contrasting approaches to discipline. When parents try to enforce two different sets of rules, kids can end up confused and frustrated. Let's take a child who likes to stay up late, for example. Dad might find himself arguing over bedtime, but Mom might be completely unbothered by her kid's night-owl ways, saying, *"My brother and I stayed up late when we were growing up, and we turned out fine. Let her make her own schedule."* Say their child has a habit of speaking disrespectfully to Mom, who then scolds—but Dad views the behavior as harmless and ignores it. In both examples, there's a lack of consistency between Mom and Dad's parenting styles that can leave their child wondering who to listen to. This issue can be even more complicated when it comes to split custody arrangements. Parents in these situations should do their best to work together to create consistency.

When kids in these inconsistent dynamics become teenagers, they often start siding with the more lenient parent and ignoring the other parent's rules. Parents do have different personalities—there's no way around that. But, presenting a united front on essential rules and boundaries should be non-negotiable. Important rules like not hitting others, speaking respectfully, and following safety guidelines (like looking both ways before crossing the street or not running with scissors) should be clearly established and consistently enforced by both parents; but they should try to reach a consensus on the smaller stuff as well, like limits on TV time. When parents operate as a team, they give children the stability they need to thrive.

Setting Effective Boundaries

- **Know Your Child**

Development varies widely among children. While some eight-year-olds can handle an hour of screen time responsibly, others may need stricter limits. Remember to set boundaries that match your child's developmental stage. You know your child's needs and capabilities best—use that understanding to help you set appropriate and effective limits.

- **Stay Consistent**

Clear, simple, and consistent rules are easier to follow. If bedtime is at 8 p.m., ensure it remains the same every night. If your child knows they must complete their homework before watching TV, stick to it. Consistently enforcing rules helps them understand expectations, providing security and self-control.

- **Allow Room for Negotiation**

Kids are more likely to follow the rules they help create. If your child isn't a big fan of math, offer choices like, *"Do you want to do your math homework before or after dinner?"* Explain the reasons behind rules, talk about expectations, and give them a chance to voice their opinions. It's also a good idea to review boundaries regularly with your child.

When you set clear boundaries and stick to them, you create a safe and supportive space where your child can focus on growing into a responsible and self-disciplined person.

Amanda and Gaurav, parents of a young son named Ben, came from different backgrounds and had conflicting disciplinary styles. Amanda believed in setting strict rules and enforcing them consistently. Gaurav, on the other hand, was more lenient, believing that kids should be free to make mistakes and learn from their experiences.

Their son Ben loved playing video games. Amanda set a rule that Ben could only play for an hour each day after finishing his homework. But Gaurav, looking back on happy memories of gaming with his siblings as a child, often told Ben it was okay to play longer. This conflicting approach left Ben confused. He didn't know whose rules to follow, leading to frequent arguments and stress in the household.

One evening, Ben forgot to finish an important homework assignment because he had spent hours playing games. Amanda was frustrated and grounded him from his console for a week. Gaurav felt this was too harsh and secretly told Ben he could play when his mom wasn't around. This inconsistency made Ben feel caught between his parents, but he followed his father's lead and gamed when his mother went out to the store. When Amanda came home, she was upset to see Ben playing his game. She threatened to ground him for another week, until Ben blurted out, "Dad said I could play when you weren't around! I never know what's right and wrong since you two always tell me different things."

Amanda and Gaurav suddenly realized the confusion and stress their differing rules were causing their son. That night when Ben went to bed, they had a serious discussion about their parenting styles and agreed on the importance of acting as a team to set clear, consistent boundaries. From then on, they decided they'd establish rules together and explain to Ben why these rules were important.

Amanda and Gaurav agreed that Ben could have his daily hour of game time, but only after completing his homework and chores. They enforced this rule consistently and included Ben in discussions about any changes or exceptions.

Once his parents began working together, Ben began to understand the importance of these boundaries and how they helped him better manage his time. With his parents operating as a team to consistently uphold clear expectations, the arguments decreased, and Ben became more responsible and cooperative. Amanda and Gaurav's united approach helped their son feel secure and supported, trusting that his parents were working together to guide him.

Quiet Time

Reflecting on the Past and Present

1. When you were a child, what rules did you have to follow at home? How did these rules impact your behavior?

   _____
   _____
   _____

2. What consequences did you face if you didn't follow the rules? Did these consequences shape how you act as a parent now?

3. Do you use any of your childhood rules in your own parenting? Why or why not?

Understanding Rules

1. Do you believe rules are essential for raising your child, or do you see them as optional guidelines? Why do you feel this way?

2. Think about the rules you've established at home. Why are they important for your child and your family?

3. Can you recall a time when your child didn't understand a rule? How did you explain it, and how could you make rules clearer in the future?

_____
_____
_____

Consistency and Fairness

1. Do you consistently enforce the rules with your child? Can you think of times when you weren't consistent? What caused the inconsistency?

_____
_____
_____

2. Do you and your husband/wife have different approaches to discipline? How do these differences affect your child, and how can you work together to present a united front?

_____
_____
_____

3. Have you ever asked your child about the fairness of your rules? What did they say, and how can you address their concerns?

Involving Your Child

1. Have you ever let your child help create any rules? How did it go?

2. Think of a time when your child broke a rule. How did you handle it, and what could you have done differently?

   How could involving your child in deciding consequences help them better understand and follow the rules?

CH10: Help Me Follow the Rules / 143

activity: "Family Rules Board"

What You'll Need:

- A poster board or chalkboard
- Markers, crayons, or chalk
- Stickers

How to Do It:

Sit down with your family, decide on a few important rules, and list the rules on the board. Let your child help decorate the board with drawings and stickers to make it fun. Hang it in a spot where everyone will see it each day, like in the kitchen or living room. Use the board to remind your child of the rules and review them together when needed.

Why It's Helpful:

This activity gives your child a sense of involvement in the rules, making them more likely to follow them. The daily reminder helps everyone remember to cooperate, and talking about the rules helps the whole family understand them better.

Phrases for Consistency and Fairness in Parenting

- "Consistency helps you know what to expect from me."
- "Fairness means everyone gets treated the same way."
- "I'm going to be fair and consistent in my decisions."
- "Consistency builds trust between us."
- "I'll stick to the rules, so you know what's expected."
- "Fairness means everyone plays by the same rules."
- "I'll be consistent with consequences for broken rules."
- "Equality means giving everyone a chance."
- "Consistency helps create a stable and secure environment."
- "I'll always listen to your side and make fair decisions."

Final Thoughts

Remember, rules aren't just about restriction and control—they're essential to provide a comfortable environment where your child can thrive. The goal is to set fair, clear, and consistent rules that provide structure to help them feel safe and learn boundaries as they grow. Since different parenting styles can lead to mixed messages that confuse kids and make boundaries hard to follow, parents should work together to agree on key rules. Consistency from both parents creates a supportive, stable environment.

CHAPTER 11

Let Me Do It!

"Do not handicap your children by making their lives easy."

—Robert A. Heinlein

I love trying things on my own, like tying my shoes or spreading jam on my toast. It's okay if I don't succeed the first time.

When I do get it right all by myself, it feels like winning a gold medal!

It can be tough to watch your child struggle. As parents, we often want to step in to save our youngsters from the sting of failure. However, allowing kids to try and sometimes fail at tasks helps build their confidence and self-reliance. In this chapter, we'll explore the importance of encouraging independence in children by letting them try things for themselves. Offering help when your child needs it is important too, of course; it's all about finding a balance between providing support and giving them the freedom to learn on their own. By finding this equilibrium, you help your child develop into a secure, independent, and self-sufficient person.

What Is Your Parenting Style?

Time for some self-reflection. Let's think about your parenting style. We'll explore a few common parenting methods here. As you read, think about which of these sounds most similar to your own approach. This will help you make necessary adjustments to encourage your child's growth.

Overprotective Parenting: Overprotective parents want to shield their children from any potential harm, failure, or disappointment. These parents have good intentions, but this approach can lead to disaster—preventing kids from learning to handle life's challenges on their own.

- **Example**: Any time your child forgets their homework, you drop everything and rush to school to deliver it. This may seem helpful in the short term, but it also ensures they never face the natural consequences of their forgetfulness and prevents them from learning responsibility and accountability.

Helicopter Parenting: Helicopter parents are overly involved in their kids' lives, micromanaging their activities and solving all their problems. This can make children feel incapable and harm their critical-thinking skills.

- **Example**: You end up taking over your child's entire science project in an effort to make sure it's perfect. Sure, the result looks great, but at what cost? Your child ends up presenting a project they barely had a hand in, missing out on the learning experience and the satisfaction of completing it on their own.

Permissive Parenting: Permissive parents are lenient to the extreme and avoid setting firm boundaries. While they are typically loving and communicative, this approach can result in their children struggling with self-discipline and boundaries.

- **Example**: Your child asks for candy right before dinner. Despite knowing it's not healthy and will likely ruin their appetite, you give in to avoid a tantrum. Caving to their demands might give your child short-term satisfaction, but the lack of structure can lead to difficulties in self-regulation and willingness to cooperate down the road.

Authoritative Parenting: Authoritative parents combine warmth and firmness, setting clear rules and expectations while remaining supportive and responsive to their children's needs. This style often leads to positive outcomes like high self-esteem and good social skills.

- **Example**: You set a rule that homework must be completed before any screen time; but you also make it clear you're available to sit down with your child and help if they're struggling. You can discuss their day and offer guidance, fostering both a sense of security and a strong emotional connection.

Take some time to reflect on these parenting styles and compare them to your own. This will help you identify areas for improvement and adopt strategies that best support your child's development.

Encouraging Independence

You may have heard terms like "helicopter parenting" or "snowplow parenting" to describe parents who hover over their children or clear every obstacle out of their way. When we parent in these ways, our intentions come from a place of love and a desire to protect our kids, but these approaches can prevent them from learning essential life skills.

Reflect on your parenting style: Are you giving your child enough opportunities to independently explore, make mistakes, and learn from them, or do you step in at the first hint of a challenge? It can be tough to recognize when to offer support and when to step back, but finding this balance is crucial for your little one's independence.

Have you ever watched your child's face light up when they figure out a tough math problem or succeed in packing their lunch by themselves? These moments build their confidence and resilience. When we do everything for our kids, we rob them of valuable opportunities to develop independence and problem-solving skills.

But when we encourage them to do things for themselves, we help them develop a strong sense of capability and self-worth. Childhood is about exploring, making mistakes, and learning from them. It's all part of the road to a confident, self-reliant future, and our job as parents is to celebrate our kids' efforts and support their growth every step of the way.

Managing Parental Anxiety

Do you feel anxious when you see your child struggling with a task? You're not alone. We all want to see our kids succeed, but stepping in too quickly can actually hold them back. Learning to manage your anxiety and letting your child try things on their own is key to their growth.

Why It's Tough to Watch

Watching your child struggle can be hard because you want to protect them from frustration or failure. But remember, challenges are important for kids; overcoming challenges on their own teaches them problem-solving skills and builds confidence.

How to Handle It

- **Pause Before Helping:** When you feel the urge to jump in, take a deep breath. Remind yourself that it's okay for your

child to struggle a little—they're learning through the process.
- **Focus on Their Growth:** Think about how overcoming challenges now will help them become more independent and resilient in the future.
- **Celebrate Effort:** Praise your child for trying, even if they don't succeed right away. This encourages them to keep going and shows that their effort is important.

Letting Them Grow

Allowing your child to try, fail, and try again helps them grow stronger and more self-reliant. By managing your anxiety, you help them on the road to becoming more confident and capable. Trust in their abilities—they'll surprise you with what they can achieve on their own.

Sofia's son Jaime always seemed indifferent about everything, especially his homework. He would often refuse to complete his assignments. Sofia couldn't bear the thought of Jaime receiving poor grades, so she often ended up doing his work for him. One afternoon, Jamie was supposed to be working on a writing assignment, but Sofia walked in to see him scrolling through videos on his tablet instead. She asked why he hadn't worked on his assignment at all, and Jaime shrugged and mumbled, "I know you'll do it for me later anyway, and you're better at writing than me." For the first time, Sofia started to realize that her impatience and habit of quickly solving her son's problems were harming his ability to learn and grow independently.

Sofia decided she needed to allow Jaime to learn to problem-solve on his own. She chose to begin by creating a boundary that Jaime was to complete his assignments on his own. At first, Jaime was frustrated and angry, not understanding why his mom wasn't helping him like before. But Sofia stood firm, determined to let Jaime tackle his homework by himself.

At first, when Jaime got stuck on a tough problem, he would complain and get upset. It was incredibly challenging for Sofia to hold back and watch him struggle, but she patiently waited for him to figure things out. Over time, Jaime began to take a more active role in his homework. His passive attitude slowly turned into a proactive one, and he started handling his assignments more independently, embracing challenges with a new sense of determination.

Sofia saw that, when given the opportunity, Jaime had the strength and capability to manage tasks on his own. Even better, Jaime realized this too, giving him a huge confidence boost. Sofia learned

the value of patience and balanced support as she watched her son become more self-reliant and capable each day.

Quiet Time

Reflecting on the Past and Present

1. As a child, did your parents often help you with tasks, or did they encourage you to do things independently? How did their approach affect your confidence in handling challenges?

2. How has your upbringing influenced the way you encourage independence in your child today?

3. Which parenting style—overprotective, helicopter, permissive, or authoritative—do you and your husband/wife most closely align with? How do you think this approach has influenced your child's development?

Encouraging Independence

1. Recall a recent time when your child wanted to do something on their own. How did you respond, and why?

2. Identify one task your child has shown an interest in doing independently. How can you support them without taking over?

Balancing Support and Independence

1. How can you create opportunities for your child to try new things while still being there if they need help?

2. When your child struggles with a task, how do you decide whether to step in or let them work through it?

3. How can you celebrate your child's efforts and resilience, even if the outcome isn't perfect? What specific actions can you take to accomplish this?

🎯 activity: "I Can Do It!" Chart

What You'll Need:

- A piece of paper or poster board
- Markers or crayons
- Stickers or stamps

How to Do It:

Create a simple chart with your child. Write down tasks they want to try on their own, like tying their shoes, making their bed, or setting the table. Let your child decorate the chart with drawings, stamps, or stickers, making it special and fun. Each time your child completes a task by themselves, they get to put a sticker or stamp next to it on the chart.

When they complete a task, make marking the chart a celebration! Give them a high-five, a hug, or a small treat to show how proud you are.

Why It's Helpful:

Watching the chart fill up helps your child feel proud and shows them how independent they are. Since the chart makes trying new tasks exciting and rewarding, this activity encourages them to try out more new things. Your positive reinforcement teaches your child that trying things on their own is important and fun.

Empowering Your Child: Positive Phrases

- "You can do it on your own—I believe in you!"
- "Try it first, and if you need help, I'm here."
- "I'm proud of you for wanting to try!"
- "You're capable of so much—give it a go!"
- "Take the lead and show me what you can do."
- "You're getting more independent every day!"
- "I love seeing you try new things and learn."
- "Give it a shot, and we'll figure it out together if needed."
- "I trust you to make good choices and do your best."
- "You're growing more confident and independent, and it's amazing to see!"

Final Thoughts

When you believe in your child, the sky is the limit for their potential! Sheltering them from failure only harms their growth. Don't worry; your child is resilient. If you let them try and fail, they will rise again. Through their attempts, kids make discoveries and learn to think critically. Explorations in their early years are steppingstones that take them down the path of strength and capability. Trust in your child's ability to overcome challenges and provide them with the support and encouragement they need to try again.

CHAPTER 12

Promises Matter

"Trust is built with consistency." —Lincoln Chafee

When you promise to take me to the park on Saturday or bake cookies together, please keep your word. When you don't, it's like dropping my ice cream on the ground. I know grown-ups are busy, but I

remember every single promise. When you keep yours, I feel special and loved.

Keeping promises to your child is important! In this chapter, we'll talk about the impact it has on the parent-child relationship. When you keep your word, you build trust and teach your little one the value of reliability and commitment. It's important to understand that even small promises matter a lot to kids, and following through fosters a sense of security and love.

Keeping Your Word

Keeping small promises might not seem like a big deal, but to your child, it means a lot. Every time you keep a promise, you're telling them, "You're important to me, and I care about what matters to you." This builds trust and reassures your child that they can depend on you; this confidence is crucial for their healthy development.

Delivered promises are like invisible threads that tie what you say to what you do. By following through, you show your child that reliability and integrity are part of being a good person. When you model this behavior, they learn to do the same.

Consider an adult example. Imagine your boss promising you a promotion after completing a big project. You work hard, meet the deadline, and deliver outstanding results. You present the completed project to your boss and excitedly wait for her to mention your promotion, but she doesn't say a word about it, and it never comes up again. How would you feel? And what would you think of your boss? You'd probably be very disappointed, and you'd likely think of your boss as untrustworthy and unreliable... or worse! A child feels similarly when a parent breaks a promise.

When you promise to go to your child's soccer game, help build a model airplane, or have a movie night, keeping these commitments, even if they seem small to you, teaches them they can count on you. The trust your child builds with you will play a huge part in how they navigate all relationships throughout their life.

Honoring your commitments is also about respect. It shows you are considerate of others, which teaches your youngster to do the same. And by sticking to your word, you show your child the respect they need to develop a healthy sense of confidence and self-worth.

It can be easy to make empty promises during a heated moment, like when you're trying to de-escalate a tantrum in the middle of a busy supermarket! It's tempting to say, "*Okay, we'll buy the toy you want next time,*" or "*If you stop crying, we'll watch your favorite movie together when we get home,*" just to get them to stop. But what happens if you don't keep those promises? Those little white lies add up, and your child might start to think they can't trust what you say. If you know you might not be able to follow through, don't make the promise in the first place.

Always do your best to keep your promises, but if you slip up, address it immediately. It's important to first explain the why, and then try to correct the situation. By owning up to your errors and making things right, you teach your child to do the same.

Remember, every promise you keep builds a little more trust. So, think before you promise, and make sure you can deliver. Ensuring your actions match your words is one of the best ways to make your child feel safe and loved, now and in the future.

Practical Tips for Keeping Promises

Promises to your child are meaningful commitments that show them how much they matter. Here are some strategies to help you make promises you can keep.

- **Set Realistic Expectations:** Only make promises you're certain you can keep. It's better to under promise and overdeliver than to risk going back on your word. For example, instead of committing to an elaborate vacation that might not be realistic, promise a smaller but realistic activity like a game night at home.

- **Involve Your Child:** Ask your child to help plan the activities you've agreed to. This manages their expectations and teaches them about commitment and contribution. Making a plan together is also great teamwork, making them feel valued and included.

- **Use Reminders:** Use tools like calendars, alarms, or reminder apps to keep track of promises. Make it a family activity to mark agreed-upon events on a calendar. This not only helps you remember but also shows your child that promises are serious business.

- **Explain Challenges:** Life is full of surprises. If circumstances come up that will make it difficult or impossible to uphold a promise, be honest with your child as soon as possible. Explain the situation and work together to reschedule. This teaches them about flexibility and problem-solving. For example, if a work emergency prevents you from taking your child to the movies as planned, explain the situation clearly and come up with a new plan.

- **Apologize When Necessary:** If you break a promise, even if it was an accident, acknowledge it and apologize sincerely. Explain why it happened and how you will prevent it in the future. This shows accountability and respect for your child's feelings. Here's what it looks like: "I'm sorry we couldn't go to the lake today. I know you were looking forward to it. Let's go tomorrow instead."

- **Celebrate Kept Promises:** When you keep a promise, celebrate a job well done together. This reinforces the importance of fulfilling commitments and makes it a memorable experience. For example, after a promised trip to the zoo, you could enjoy a special treat together and talk about the highlights of the day.

By using these tips to help keep yourself honest and consistent, you build a strong, trusting bond with your child that will serve as a foundation for their future relationships.

One evening, Jack excitedly asked his daughter, Kaylee, "Once I've answered the rest of these emails, how about going for a bike ride?" Kaylee rolled her eyes and responded with an indifferent "Whatever." Surprised by her reaction, Jack asked why she was upset. Kaylee, visibly frustrated, replied, *"You always say things like that, but you never keep your promises. I doubt this time will be any different."* Jack didn't want to admit it, but Kaylee was right. This got him thinking about the importance of the promises he made to his daughter and how often he failed to keep them.

Determined to make things different this time, Jack finished his work early, knocked on Kaylee's door, and said, *"Let's go biking."* Kaylee's face lit up with surprise and joy. They went for a long ride around the neighborhood and had a wonderful time together. The next day, Kaylee asked if they could spend time together again. Jack agreed and told her he would help her with the birdhouse she'd been wanting to build after finishing his work. An hour later, he kept his promise, and they spent the afternoon building and painting the birdhouse together.

As Jack made it a point to start keeping his promises, Kaylee began to trust him more. She stopped complaining and patiently

waited whenever Jack asked her to. Over time, their bond grew stronger, and Kaylee knew she could rely on her father's word. Jack realized that keeping promises, no matter how small, was vital in building a trusting and loving relationship with his daughter.

Quiet Time

Reflecting on the Past and Present

1. Were your parents generally good at keeping the promises they made? How did their consistency (or lack of it) affect your trust in them?

2. Do you remember a specific promise your parents didn't keep? How did it make you feel?

3. How do you think the way your parents handled promises has influenced how you handle them with your children?

Understanding the Impact of Promises

1. Think about a recent promise you kept to your child. How did your child react?

2. How does keeping promises affect your child's trust and confidence in you?

Building Consistency and Trust

1. What strategies can you use to make sure you keep the promises you make to your child? Could reminders, a promise journal, or other tools help?

2. What are some ways to make them feel valued and respected?

3. How can you explain to your child when you can't keep a promise, and what can you do to make it up to them, so they still trust you?

# activity: The Promise Jar

What You'll Need:

- A jar or container
- Paper strips
- A pen

⇨ **How to Do It:**

When you or your child make a promise, write it on a piece of paper. "I promise to play a game with you on Saturday," for example. Then fold up the paper and put it in your jar to serve as a reminder of the promise. Once a week, take all the strips of paper out of the jar and look at them together. Talk about the promises you kept and how this made you feel, and celebrate together with a hug, a high-five, or a small treat. If a promise wasn't kept, explain why and make a plan to keep it soon.

⇨ **Why It Helps:**

This is a great activity to build trust, encourage communication, and create positive memories.

Positive Phrases to Encourage Consistency

- "When I promise something to you, I make sure to follow through."
- "Keeping my word shows you that you can trust me."
- "Every promise I keep brings us closer."
- "I strive to be consistent because it builds trust between us."
- "You can count on me to keep my promises."
- "I will always try my best to keep my word."
- "Our promises to each other matter, and I will honor them."
- "Keeping promises shows respect and builds our relationship."
- "I value your trust and will do my best to keep my promises."
- "When I say I'll do something, I mean it, and I'll do my best to follow through."

Final Thoughts

Remember, even the smallest promise still matters to your child. Make sure you do everything in your power to uphold your word when you commit to something; only make promises you know you can keep. The temporary relief of getting through a difficult moment with an empty promise can lead to a broken heart—and a broken sense of trust—for your little one. Consistently keeping your word builds confidence and shows your child how much you love them, all while teaching them the importance of integrity and reliability in all relationships

CHAPTER 13

"Time spent playing with children is never wasted."

—Dawn Lantero

Spending time together, whether we're building forts or pretending we're on a moon mission, is the best! Even if it's just for five or ten minutes, the moments we share make me feel super special and close to you. These happy memories make me a happy kid.

Quality time with you fills your child with joy! Intentional connection is way more than just being physically present; it means taking an active part in interacting with your child through engaging activities and play. Let's explore how to build a solid bond, boost your child's confidence, and create lasting memories by making the most of these precious moments.

Quality Time, Happy Kid

The Harvard Study of Adult Development and the American Academy of Pediatrics agree: If you want happy kids, play with them as much as you can! Sounds simple, right? But, as any busy parent knows, it's not always that easy. Out of love, many parents misguidedly try to financially compensate their kids for this lack of time. They buy the latest video games, newest tech gadgets, shiniest bikes, and fanciest dolls. But what your kids really want from you is *you*—your presence.

✓ What is Your Definition of Quality Time?

What does "quality time" mean to you? Your definition can make a big difference. For example, if you catch up on social media while sitting next to your child who is watching videos on their iPad, would you call that quality time? Sure, those moments can be fine, but let's think about what true bonding time really means. It's giving your child your full focus and engaging in meaningful ways that show them they're the center of your world.

The Importance of Quality Time

Every special moment you spend with your child is like a precious photo in the memory book of your relationship, and each one helps you grow closer. When you make time just for you and your child, you're giving them a strong feeling of being loved and valued. This meaningful time serves as a reminder that you are present, nurturing your little one's sense of security.

Quality time can also be practical—you can use it as a chance to teach important life skills. Through play and conversations, kids learn how to communicate, understand others' feelings, and solve problems. These interactions are a learning experience for you, too, helping you better understand your child and support their growth.

And this isn't just wishful thinking; these benefits are backed by research. According to a study by Harvard University, children who spend regular quality time with their parents perform better in school, develop stronger social skills, and have fewer behavioral problems. Quality time is so important that family meals and shared activities are recommended by the American Academy of Pediatrics as a way to foster emotional security and overall well-being in children.

- **Reducing Behavior Problems**

If you're looking for a way to encourage good behavior, try making special moments a priority. When kids feel understood and connected with their parents, they are less likely to act out to get attention—and more likely to be cooperative and adaptable.

- **Make the Most of Your Time**

Remember—true to its name, quality time is about the quality of the moments you spend with your child, not the quantity! Making the most of the moments you share makes your home a loving, supportive, and happy place for your child to grow. So put down the phone and enjoy some real bonding time together!

Overcoming Common Challenges

When you're juggling work, chores, and everything else that needs to get done, finding time to play with your child can be tough! Many parents struggle with this and might even feel guilty when they can't spend as much time as they'd like with their kids. But you're not alone There are ways to make it work, even on your busiest days.

- **Start Small:** You don't need to set aside hours for playtime. Even just 10 to 15 minutes of focused, uninterrupted play can make a big difference to your child. These short, special moments add up and help build a strong bond. Whether it's a quick game of catch or reading a short story together, what matters most is that you're fully present during this time. So, unplug from devices and focus on your little one.

- **Incorporate Play into Daily Routines:** Scheduling playtime doesn't have to be complicated—it can be built right into your daily routine. You can turn everyday tasks into fun activities, so get creative. For example, let your child help with cooking by washing vegetables or stirring ingredients. Bathtime can become an aquatic adventure with toys and games, and bedtime can be extra special with make-believe stories. These small changes can turn ordinary tasks into chances to connect.

- **Set Realistic Expectations:** It's important to be kind to yourself and stay realistic. Some days you'll be too tired or busy for long play sessions, and that's okay. Instead of focusing on what you can't do, celebrate what you can—what matters most are the moments you can share with your child. Remember, it's the quality of the time you spend together that counts, not the quantity. On those particularly busy days, even a few minutes of laughter or a quick game can go a long way.

- **Make Playtime a Priority:** To make sure playtime happens, treat it like any other important part of your day. Schedule it in, whether it's a quick game before dinner or a playful round of jokes during a car ride. When you make playtime a regular part of your routine, it becomes something you and your child look forward to every day.

It's okay to recognize the challenges modern life poses to quality time with our kids. By finding ways to weave play into your daily life, you can build meaningful connections with your child without feeling overwhelmed. Remember, it's the little, consistent efforts that make the biggest difference in your little one's happiness and growth.

Tips for Integrating Playtime

Play can be one of the best—and most fun—ways to connect with your child. But fitting it into a busy schedule can sometimes be easier said than done. Here are some practical tips to help you integrate playtime into your daily routine:

Morning Routine

- Wake-Up Play: Energize yourselves and start the morning on a fun note with a quick game like *Simon Says* or a five-minute dance party to your child's favorite song.
- Breakfast Bonding: Make breakfast enjoyable by playing a simple game like *I Spy* or sharing jokes over your meal.

Transition Times

- Before Dinner: Make dinner prep fun by pretending you're running a five-star restaurant! While cooking, give your child tasks to do, like washing vegetables or setting the table.
- After Homework: Hard work pays off—reward your child with a ten-minute game like *Hide and Seek* after they finish

their studies. This is a great way to transition from work to play!

Bedtime Routine

- Wind-Down Play: Engaging in calm activities before sleep helps your little one relax while having fun. Try building with blocks, playing with plushies, or drawing together.
- Storytime Adventures: Level up your bedtime stories by using different voices for characters or letting your child decide how the story progresses in a choose-your-own-adventure fashion.

On-the-Go Play

- Car Games: Entertain your child without screens during travel time by playing simple games like *20 Questions* or the *Alphabet Game*—or use the time to make up fun stories together.
- Waiting Time: Simple activities like *Tic-Tac-Toe* or a game of *Go Fish* can make waiting more bearable. Take the doctor's office waiting room from a bore to a blast by bringing along portable toys, a deck of cards, or a notebook and pens.

Weekend Fun

- Family Playtime: Create a routine everyone will look forward to by setting aside a specific time each weekend for family play. Brainstorm with your little one on each weekend's activities, like visiting the park, biking, or baking cookies together.
- Special Activities: Start a cherished family tradition like "Saturday Morning Crafts." Choose a simple DIY project,

like making a wreath or painting rocks, to complete together.

Making Playtime Special

- Stay Consistent: Try to schedule playtime at around the same time each day, like right after dinner or before bedtime. A consistent playtime routine gives your child something to look forward to, motivating them throughout their day.
- Follow Their Lead: Let your child choose the activity sometimes! Whether it's playing with their favorite toys or coming up with a game, following their lead shows you value their interests.
- Be Present: Unplug during playtime by ditching distractions like phones and the TV. This is your time together, so give your child your undivided attention.

Life gets busy! By incorporating these practical tips, you can fit playtime into your daily routine and create memories that you and your child will cherish for a lifetime.

David sometimes found it challenging to unplug from his work and household chores to connect with his young son Ethan. Because his father wasn't big on play while he was growing up, the concept didn't always come naturally to David. Even so, David was a dedicated father, so when Ethan started coming home from school each day feeling irritable and frustrated, he knew he needed to get to the bottom of it.

He started by sitting down with Ethan over dinner and asking how school was going. *"I feel bored, Dad,"* Ethan sighed, propping his elbow on the table and resting his chin in his hand. *"It feels like all I do is go to school, come home and sleep, and do it all over again the next day."* Ethan's frustration brought back memories of David's own childhood and the boredom he felt when his dad was too busy to play with him. He wanted to help his son feel like a kid again. Determined to build a better bond with Ethan but unsure where to start, David searched for playtime ideas online. He made a list of activities to try out and decided to dedicate 15minutes a day to playing with his son.

At first, playtime felt forced and awkward for David. He had to push himself to get on the floor and act silly, something that didn't come naturally to him. But as he saw the joy light up Ethan's eyes and smile, he began to understand the importance of his commitment. They started with simple activities like building forts in the living room, pretending to be explorers on a big adventure, and playing tag outside. Despite David's initial discomfort, thanks to Ethan's joyful laughter, he started to loosen up. His son's happiness was contagious, and David began to feel the joy of these interactions as well.

The impact of those 15minutes extended beyond their playtime. David noticed that Ethan became much more cooperative at home, and his grades even improved. Now that he had quality time with his dad to look forward to every day, Ethan's motivation skyrocketed.

One evening, after a stressful day at work, a worn-out David was tempted to skip their playtime. But when he saw the eager look in Ethan's eyes, he pushed his exhaustion aside. That night, as they played superheroes, David realized how important these moments were—not just for Ethan but for himself. The stress melted away, replaced by laughter and connection.

David learned that even a brief, daily moment of focused attention could make his son's heart happy. What started as an act of service for his son quickly became the best part of both of their days—memories in the making.

Quiet Time

Reflecting on the Past and Present

1. Did your parents spend time playing with you when you were a child? What kinds of games did you enjoy together?

2. What are your fondest memories of playing with your parents? How did those moments impact your relationship?

3. How have your parents' ideas of quality time influenced your interactions with your child?

Prioritizing Quality Time

1. How much time do you typically spend playing with your child each day? Do you feel it's enough to build a strong connection?

2. Do you let your child choose the activities during playtime, or do you usually take the lead? Which approach do they enjoy more?

3. Have you ever introduced new games or activities during playtime? How did your child respond to the change?

Recognizing the Importance of Play

1. What are your child's favorite games? How do these games contribute to their growth and happiness?

2. Ask your child what they enjoy most about playing with you. What can you learn from their answer to improve your playtime together?

Building Strong Connections

1. When was the last time you had a memorable play session with your child? What made it special?

2. Plan a unique playtime activity that you can both enjoy. How can you make it a fun and memorable experience?

🎯 Activity: Our Playtime Plan

Work with your child to create a weekly playtime plan. Together, list activities you both enjoy, like building forts, playing board games, or going on imaginary adventures. Let your child decorate the plan with drawings or stickers to make it special. Each day, choose one activity from the list to focus on.

Hang your playtime plan somewhere visible, like on the fridge, to give you both something to look forward to every day. This plan helps ensure that you're dedicating time to play each day and lets your child know that their happiness and fun are a priority.

☺ Quotes about Quality Time

- "The best investment we can make is in the time we spend with our children."

- "In the end, kids won't remember the things we bought them but the time we spent with them."
- "Every moment we spend with our children is a gift that creates memories to last a lifetime."
- "Our children need our presence more than presents."
- "Time spent with our kids is never wasted; it's an investment in their future."
- "The quality of our time with our kids is more important than the quantity."
- "The most precious gift we can give our children is our time and attention."
- "Time spent with our kids strengthens our bond and builds a foundation of trust and love."
- "As parents, our most important job is being there for our kids, no matter what."

Final Thoughts

Of course, parenting is exhausting and challenging at times but remember that children grow up quickly. One moment they're starting middle school, and the next, they're graduating high school. Before you know it, you're giving them a ride to college. By then, it's too late to regret not spending more time playing with them when they were little. Now, while you have the chance, dedicate your heart to playing with your children. Even if you only set aside 10 to 15 minutes a day for play, those moments of joy and genuine engagement will stay with them, filling their memories with happiness and love.

CHAPTER 14

Fair Consequences

"Fair consequences teach children responsibility and respect without breaking their spirit." —Unknown

When a punishment is too long or too tough, it feels too hard—and I feel like giving up. So, if I forget to put my toys away once, please don't take them away for a whole month. If it's just for a few

days, I'll understand better and try harder next time. I want to learn from my mistakes, but I need you to help by making the consequences fair.

It's important to be reasonable when it comes to discipline. Fair consequences should match the behavior and be manageable for your child. In this chapter, we'll explore how to help them learn from their mistakes without causing resentment or resistance.

Setting Reasonable Consequences

When kids make mistakes, parents often react impulsively with the first consequence that comes to mind. When your judgment is clouded with negative emotions like anger, you can't effectively discipline your child—and trying to do so often results in poor outcomes. Think about your reactions: If your child breaks a picture frame while playing, how do you respond? Do you take a deep breath and think things through, or do you automatically yell and ground them? This chapter encourages you to rethink your criteria for disciplining your child.

How Long Should Punishment Last?

When children misbehave, they need consequences that they can realistically follow without feeling unfairly treated. Punishments that are too severe or last too long can backfire. As they say, the punishment should fit the crime, or in this case, the misbehavior.

- **Example:** Your child refuses to wear a helmet while riding their bike. You decide to ban them from riding their bike for a month. While this consequence is related to their behavior, it is excessively harsh and likely to result in negative feelings. Instead, consider a more reasonable duration, such as restricting bike riding for a week. This shorter duration still sends a clear message about the importance of safety without making your child feel unreasonably punished.

- **Practical Tip:** Always match the duration of the consequence to the severity of the behavior. Consider your child's age and ability to comprehend the lesson you're teaching. This approach will help them understand the connection between their actions and the consequences.

Connecting Actions and Consequences

Equally important is ensuring that the consequence is directly related to the behavior. Unrelated punishments can confuse your child and fail to teach the intended lesson.

- **Example:** Your child refuses to wear their bike helmet, and you react by taking away their tablet for a week. This punishment is totally disconnected from their original misbehavior. Instead, relate the consequence to the specific action. In this case, a suitable consequence would be "no bike riding for a week." This way, you directly tie the punishment to the safety issue, making it clear to your child why their behavior was problematic.

- **Practical Tip:** Before deciding on a consequence, make sure it is logical and directly related to the poor behavior. This helps your child understand the connection between their actions and the outcome, making it more likely they'll comply and learn from the situation.

Hassan and Amir's Story

Hassan and his son Amir frequently struggled with their bedtime routine. Amir loved playing with his toys before bed and would often refuse to put them away when it was time to sleep. When Amir refused to clean up, Hassan usually responded by canceling Amir's weekend trips to the park. This punishment typically caused Amir to go into a full-blown tantrum—and over time, he became increasingly defiant, often breaking rules intentionally out of frustration.

One night, another argument began about Amir's toys. Hassan lashed out without thinking, threatening to take away Amir's weekend park trip. This time unbothered, Amir responded, *"You already took away the park trip last night, Dad, so it doesn't even matter if I pick up my toys now. I don't care anymore anyway; I'll just play with my toys on the weekend instead."* Hassan suddenly realized that the consequences he set for Amir's behavior weren't teaching him the right lessons. They were confusing and frustrating his son since he couldn't see the connection between his misbehavior and the punishment.

Hassan decided to change his method. Instead of impulsively canceling park trips in anger, he began explaining to Amir the importance of keeping his room tidy. He set a new rule: *"If you don't put your toys away before bed, you won't be able to play with them the next day."* This new consequence was directly related to the behavior, and Amir understood why it was necessary.

The next evening, when Amir left his toys out again, Hassan calmly enforced the rule. Amir was disappointed with the consequences but accepted the punishment without tantrums or resistance. After a while, he began putting his toys away without being asked, understanding the relationship between his actions and consequences. Amir began to recognize the importance of tidiness; he realized he enjoyed being able to find a specific toy with ease when his room was organized. Once Amir saw his father's discipline as fair and related to his actions, their relationship grew stronger.

🔨 How to Teach Through Consequences

✓ Keep It Short and Manageable

Long, drawn-out punishments only make kids feel overwhelmed and defeated. Picture how disheartening it would be to lose something you love for a long time. Shorter durations keep the lesson impactful without overwhelming or discouraging your little one, so keep your consequences short and consistent for the most effective results.

- **Example:** Your child refuses to do their homework and instead watches videos on their tablet. You consider taking their tablet away for three weeks but ultimately decide to limit it to a few days. Your child can see the end of the punishment in sight and feels motivated to improve their behavior.

✓ Explain Clearly

Make sure your child understands why they're being disciplined. Clear explanations help them connect their behavior to the consequences. When kids see the reason behind rules and consequences, they're more likely to cooperate. It's like connecting the dots for them, making the lesson more meaningful.

- **Example:** Your child doesn't clean up their art supplies when you ask. You say, *"We need to clean up art supplies after using them because a tidy space is safe and pleasant for everyone. If they are not put away, we won't be able to play with them tomorrow."*

✓ Consistency is Key

Stick to the rules you set. Consistent consequences help kids understand what's expected of them and build trust in your words.

- **Example:** You have a household rule about completing homework before allowing screen time, and you enforce it every day. Consistency helps your child learn what's expected, creating a stable environment where they feel secure. They know you mean what you say, building a sense of reliability.

Quiet Time

Reflecting on the Past and Present

1. Think back to when you were a kid. Were there any punishments that felt unfair? How did they affect you?

   _____
   _____
   _____

2. Recall a recent time you gave your child a consequence. Was it fair and related to what they did? How did your child react, and did it help them learn from their mistake?

Planning Fair Consequences

1. List some common misbehaviors in your home. What fair consequences can you set for each one?

2. How can you clearly explain to your child why they're receiving a specific consequence?

Understanding the Impact

1. After you give a consequence, how does your child usually respond? Do they understand why it's happening, or do they seem confused and upset?

2. Have you noticed any differences in your child's behavior when you use fair consequences instead of harsher ones? What are those differences?

Activity: "Cause and Effect" Cards

Sit down with your child and make a set of cards together. On one side of each card, write down a potential misbehavior, like, "Not putting toys away." On the other side of the card, write down the consequences for the behavior, like, "No toys the next day."

Once you've made your cards, go through them with your child. Talk about why the consequence for each action makes sense. For example, if they don't put their toys away, they won't be able to play with them the next day because it's important to keep a tidy home.

Here are a few examples of "Cause and Effect" cards:

Card 1:

- **Front Side (Cause):** "Leaving art supplies out after using them."
- **Back Side (Effect):** "No art supplies tomorrow."

Card 2:

- **Front Side (Cause):** "Not finishing homework."
- **Back Side (Effect):** "No TV time until homework is done."

Card 3:

- **Front Side (Cause):** "Refusing to share the tablet with a sibling."
- **Back Side (Effect):** "No screen time for the rest of the day."

Card 4:

- **Front Side (Cause):** "Talking back to parents."
- **Back Side (Effect):** "No playdate this weekend."

Card 5:

- **Front Side (Cause):** "Eating junk food right before dinner."
- **Back Side (Effect):** "No junk food the next day."

This activity helps your child see how their actions lead to consequences. By making the cards together, your child will better understand the rules and feel like they're part of the process. Plus, it's a fun way to learn important lessons about responsibility!

Final Thoughts

When it comes to discipline, being fair and reasonable is key. When we're angry, it's easy to give out punishments that are too harsh and seem unjust. If kids think a punishment is unfair, they won't learn from it. Always think about why you're giving a punishment and make sure the severity matches the offense. This way, you respect your child while teaching them a valuable lesson.

CHAPTER 15

Screen Time Struggles

"Technology is a useful servant but a dangerous master." — Christian Lous Lange

Please don't yell at me or snatch my tablet away when I spend too much time on it. It's super frustrating to me, especially when I'm about to win a game! I will listen better if you use a gentle

reminder first. I know I often refuse to turn it off, but I'll try if you do too.

As any modern parent knows, screen time can be tough to manage—let's explore some effective strategies that can help. The goal is to find a balance that allows your child to enjoy technology responsibly while still having enough time for important activities like physical play, socializing, and family time. By setting clear boundaries and using gentle reminders, you can help your child develop healthy screen habits without all the conflict.

Understanding the Issue

Nowadays, kids and adults both struggle to control their screen time. Children are naturally drawn to the bright colors, sounds, and instant rewards that screens provide, making it easy for them to get hooked. Screen time addiction isn't just a minor inconvenience; it can have serious consequences like disrupted sleep patterns, reduced physical activity, and impaired social skills. Children's performance in school can also suffer when they put screen time before homework and studying. Screens provide nearly constant stimulation, which can shorten kids' attention spans and make managing boredom a struggle.

Not all online content is appropriate or beneficial, so it's important to be aware of what your child views on their devices. Social media is full of unrealistic standards and can be a haven for cyberbullying, and certain games and videos can promote violence or unhealthy behaviors.

As parents, our role is to model healthy technology use and guide our children in finding a balance. Understanding these issues can help us make informed decisions about setting limits and encourage the diverse activities a healthy childhood needs. Let's dive into some proactive steps to mitigate the risks of screen time.

Taming Excessive Electronic Use

Phones, tablets, gaming consoles—oh my! With all the electronic devices available today, it doesn't take much effort for a kid—or an adult—to spend too much time behind a screen. Banning devices and the internet entirely isn't a realistic solution for most families, so we must promote a well-rounded lifestyle by guiding our kids in developing healthy screen habits. Here are some practical tips to achieve this.

✓ Set Clear Rules

Setting consistent limits and rules around screen time can be easier said than done. Picture this: Screen time is over, but your little one isn't ready to give up the phone. Now you're wondering if you should pry it out of your screaming child's hands or if you should give in and let them keep watching. Sound familiar? Just like we discussed in Chapter 10, the key to effective rule-setting is involving your child. When they have a hand in creating the rules, they are more likely to stick to them. Discuss and agree on time limits together - one hour on school nights and two hours on weekend nights, for example. Talk about why these rules matter, and make sure your child understands the importance of filling their day with a variety of activities. When they have a say and understand why the rule is needed, they are less likely to push back when reminded to stick to it.

✓ Gentle Reminders

Instead of yelling at them to put the tablet away or snatching it out of their hands, use gentle reminders when screen time is coming to a close. Give your child a heads-up like, *"You have ten more minutes to play, and then it's time to turn off the tablet."* If they resist or talk back, you can continue with, *"Remember, if you don't follow the rule, we agreed that there will be no tablet time tomorrow."* This respects their need for transition time while highlighting the importance of sticking to the rules, making them more likely to cooperate.

✓ Encouraging Alternative Activities

Busy and exhausted parents are often tempted to tell children to play on their own, causing them to quickly get bored and start begging for the TV or tablet. You can avoid this by engaging your child in activities that naturally promote hobbies like reading, sports, or arts and crafts. Local libraries and community centers can also be huge assets; they often offer free classes for children, so explore these resources and take advantage of them. When you introduce your child to fun and interactive hobbies that keep them entertained, you'll reduce their reliance on screens.

✓ Consistency is Key

Throughout this book, we've learned about the importance of consistency. Still, it can be easy to find excuses not to stick to the guidelines we set, especially during tough moments. This might look like letting your child use the tablet a little longer than usual while you wrap up dinner with guests or to keep them busy during grocery shopping. Sure, some flexibility is necessary depending on the situation, but consistently bending the rules can send mixed messages. Maybe you give the phone back every time your child throws a tantrum; this can teach them that acting out will get them what they want. Setting rules is important, but sticking to them is even more crucial. When you maintain consistency, your little one will learn to understand and respect boundaries.

✓ Leading by Example

Be an example when it comes to screen time. Remember: *"Monkey See, Monkey Do"*—children mimic the behaviors they observe. When you tell your child to read a book while your own eyes are glued to your phone, your words lose impact. Model balanced screen habits of your own by sticking to time limits and putting away devices while spending time together. Show them that other activities, like reading or playing outside, are valuable and enjoyable. Your healthy behavior will guide your child toward healthier screen time habits of their own.

How to Earn Screen Time

Managing screen time can be a real challenge, but one way to make it easier for your child is by having them earn their screen time. When they have an active part in deciding how much screen time they get, it helps them set personal limits and encourages them to engage in other important activities. It's a simple system that teaches responsibility and balance, which can make a big difference in their daily routine.

Why It Works: Kids love having a sense of control, and when they can earn something they enjoy—like screen time, they're more motivated to complete other tasks. This method helps them understand that screen time is a reward for their efforts, not an automatic right. It also makes them more aware of how they're spending their time, encouraging a healthy mix of activities.

How To Set It Up:

- **Clear and Simple Tasks:** Start by picking a few tasks that your child can do to earn screen time. These could be things like doing their homework, helping with chores, or spending time playing outside. For example, *"Finish your homework without being reminded, and you can earn thirty minutes of screen time."*

- **Create a Chart:** Make a simple chart your child can use to track the tasks they've completed. Each time they finish a task, they earn a sticker or a point, which they can trade in for screen time. Keep the chart somewhere visible, like on the fridge, so they can see their progress and stay motivated.

- **Encourage Screen-Free Activities:** Reward activities that don't involve screens, like reading a book, playing with toys, or doing something creative. Here's what this looks like: *"Spend thirty minutes reading, and you can earn fifteen minutes of screen time."*

- **Set Limits:** Even with this system, don't throw screen time limits out the window. Put a cap on how much screen time your child can earn in a day or week, and make sure they are aware of the limit. Even if they've earned it, you don't want your little one spending too much time in front of a screen.

- **Positive Reinforcement:** Praise your child when they follow the system. A simple *"Great job earning your screen time today!"* can go a long way. This positive feedback encourages them to keep up the good work.

Making It Work: Involve your child in the process when setting up a system to earn screen time. Let them help decide which tasks will earn screen time and how much each task is worth. This way, they'll feel more invested and be more likely to stick to it.

Jennifer, a busy working mom, often found herself relying on screens to keep her kids entertained. After a long day at work, she would hand them their tablets or turn on the TV so she could prepare dinner and relax. This gave her a moment of peace while she cooked, but it usually ended in more stress—her kids would often throw tantrums and refuse to turn off the devices to eat dinner.

One day, Jennifer came across an article about unrestricted screen time. She noticed some similarities to her own situation and realized that the tantrums and resistance were likely a result of her kids' screen habits. She decided to make a change by trying out some of the tips in the article. Jennifer began offering her children a choice: they could either watch TV or play with their tablets for forty-five minutes while she cooked, or they could engage in another activity like playing with toys. If they chose screen time, she set a timer and gently reminded them when the time was almost up.

When the timer went off, at first, her kids complained that the time was too short. But Jennifer remained consistent, she explained why the new rules were important and stuck to them. Slowly but surely, the tantrums lessened, and her kids began to understand and accept the limits. They got used to the timer and started to anticipate when it would go off, helping them transition to dinner time without as much fuss.

Consistency was key for Jennifer. There were days when she wavered and allowed more screen time, and she noticed it led to confusion and resistance. But when she consistently enforced the rules, her kids adapted, found other ways to entertain themselves, and became more cooperative. Jennifer also noticed that playfully involving her children in small tasks, like setting the table, helped them feel engaged and less focused on their screens.

This newfound structure reduced power struggles and led to a more relaxed and stress-free atmosphere at home. Jennifer's evenings went more smoothly, and her kids learned the importance of balancing healthy screen time with other activities.

Quiet Time

Reflecting on Past and Present

1. When you were growing up, did you have TV screen time? How many hours were you allowed to watch per day? How did your parents react when you watched more than allowed?

   _____
   _____
   _____

2. How do you think your childhood screen time habits influence how you manage your child's screen time now?

3. Recall a recent screen time conflict. How did you handle it, and what could you do differently next time?

Planning Screen Time

1. Based on your child's age, what are reasonable daily and weekly screen time limits? How will you explain these limits to your child?

2. How can you use gentle reminders to help your child transition from screen time to another activity?

3. Identify alternative activities your child enjoys. How can you encourage these activities more often?

Encouraging Healthy Habits

1. How can you ensure screen time rules are consistent and clear for your child?

2. Reflect on a time when you successfully managed screen time without conflict. What strategies worked well?

🎯 Activity 1: Screen-Free Fun

Let's take a break from the screens and try out some fun activities you and your child can do together:

Indoor Play

- **Get Creative:** Grab some paper and crayons, markers, or paint, and let your and your child's imagination run wild. Whether it's drawing or crafting, it's a great way to bond and spark creativity.
- **Reading Corner:** Set up a cozy spot where you and your child can dive into a good book. This is a simple way to build their love for reading.
- **Family Game Time:** Pull out a board game or puzzle and enjoy some screen-free family time. Perfect for learning and laughing together!

Outdoor Activities

- **Take a Walk:** Go for a walk in the park or around your neighborhood. It's a nice way to get some fresh air and take in the sights.
- **Get Active:** Kick a ball around, play catch, or have a race. Outdoor play is great for kids' health and lots of fun, too!
- **Start a Garden:** Plant some flowers or veggies together and enjoy the reward of watching your hard work grow.

Keep Track with a Fun Chart

- **Make a Chart:** Create a simple chart to track all the screen-free activities your child does. Let them add a sticker or checkmark each time they complete an activity. It's a fun way to keep them motivated and be proud of their efforts.

🎯 Activity 2: "Earn Your Screen Time" Chart

Create an "Earn Your Screen Time" chart with your child. Together, pick some tasks they can do to earn screen time, like finishing homework, reading, or helping with chores. For each task they complete, let them add a sticker or checkmark to the chart. Once they reach a certain number, they can enjoy their screen time for the day.

This activity makes earning screen time fun and helps your child learn about balance and responsibility. It's a simple way to encourage healthy habits and show them how to mix screen time with other important activities.

Final Thoughts

The goal of controlling screen time shouldn't be to ban devices but to teach your child to use them responsibly. Like all things in life, it's about balance. You can help them develop healthy screen habits by setting clear rules, giving gentle reminders, and offering engaging and diverse alternative activities. Talk with your little one and come up with screen time hours together; they'll be more likely to cooperate if they have a say and understand the reasons behind the rules.

Reflection

As we reach the final pages of *A Letter from Your Child*, it's time to reflect on the practical strategies and tools we've gathered along the way. Parenting is an ever-evolving journey, and while there's no perfect roadmap, having a solid toolbox can help us navigate the ups and downs.

Throughout this book, we've explored ideas and methods that can deepen your connection with your child while also supporting their emotional development. Here's a quick reminder of the essential tools you now have at your fingertips:

- **Listening and Communication Tools**
  Active listening opens up meaningful conversations. By engaging in your child's world, you build trust and understanding. Keep asking open-ended questions and offering your full attention during those special moments.

- **Gentle Discipline Tools**
  You've learned the value of setting fair, manageable

consequences and approaching discipline with calmness. This not only helps your child learn from their mistakes but also encourages them to grow with confidence.

- **Screen Time Management Tools**
  Balancing screen time can be a challenge, but with clear boundaries, gentle reminders, and engaging alternatives, you can guide your child towards healthier habits without the struggle.

- **Play and Quality Time Tools**
  Play is the language of children. Even a few minutes of undivided attention can work wonders for your relationship. Letting your child lead playtime shows them that you cherish these moments together.

- **Promise-Keeping Tools**
  Your words and actions matter. By keeping your promises, no matter how small, you reinforce the foundation of trust that your child relies on.

As you move forward, think of these tools as stepping stones to a more connected, calm, and joyful parenting experience. Every day presents new opportunities to practice, grow, and improve.

Conclusion

Embracing the Journey Together

Dear Fellow Parents,

Congratulations on taking this journey with me through "A Letter from Your Child." I hope these pages have offered a fresh perspective on the incredible role you play in your child's life.

Remember, parenting isn't about perfection—it's about connection, understanding, and love. Embrace every moment, with its highs and lows, as an opportunity for growth for both you and your child.

Let's promise to celebrate our children's unique sparks, offer them unconditional love, and view the world through their curious eyes. Together, let's nurture future adults who are empathetic, resilient, and overflowing with self-worth.

Here's to every beautiful, messy, and miraculous moment of parenthood. Let's make this journey a heartfelt adventure—one loving look, one encouraging word, one warm hug at a time.

Let's be their unwavering support in times of need and, most importantly, their constant source of love.

Parenting is the most profound symphony we'll ever compose. Let's make it a masterpiece filled with harmony, love, and resilience. Together, let's create a world where our children feel seen, heard, and deeply cherished.

Thank you for embarking on this journey with me. Let's continue to make beautiful music, one heartfelt note at a time.

With love and warmth,

Carrie Khang

If any part of this book made you pause, reflect, or feel a little less alone as a parent, I would love to hear from you.

Your words matter — not just to me, but to another parent who may need to read exactly what you have to say.

If it feels right, please consider leaving a review.

Thank you for being part of this journey.
I truly appreciate your support.

Resources

1. **The Junior School**, "The Importance of Boundaries." *ESMS*, December 2021. https://www.esms.org.uk/news/importance-boundaries
2. **Prabha, S. Divya.** "Scolding Your Child to Discipline Him? Parents, Know Your Limits." *Parent Circle*. https://www.parentcircle.com/effects-of-parents-scolding-a-child/article
3. **Wolf, Jennifer.** "Why Shaming Your Kids Isn't Effective Discipline." *Verywell Family*, January 2022. https://www.verywellfamily.com/why-you-shouldnt-shame-your-children-4089277
4. **Jensen, Alexander C., and Susan M. McHale.** "What Makes Siblings Different? The Development of Sibling Differences in Academic Achievement and Interests." *Journal of Family Psychology, 29*, no. 3 (2015): 469–478. https://willingness.com.mt/the-effects-of-comparing-siblings/

www.ingramcontent.com/pod-product-compliance
Lightning Source LLC
Chambersburg PA
CBHW020247010526
44107CB00002B/135